# CARE FOR THE NEURODIVERGENT SOUL

*Wired Differently. Living Intentionally.*

DIANNE A. ALLEN, MA

VISIONS APPLIED

**Copyright © 2025 by Dianne A. Allen**
All rights reserved.

No part of this publication may be reproduced, distributed, or transmitted in any form or by any means, including photocopying, recording, or other electronic or mechanical methods, without the prior written permission of the publisher, except in the case of brief quotations embodied in critical reviews and certain other noncommercial uses permitted by copyright law.

For permission requests, write to the publisher at:
**Visions Applied, LLC**
www.visionsapplied.com

**ISBN:** 978-0-9995778-7-5 (Paperback)
978-1-968943-00-4 (Hardcover)
978-0-9995778-8-2 (eBook)

**Library of Congress Control Number:** 2025912576

Cover design by Nic Albright
Interior design by Clark Kenyon
Printed in the United States of America

First Edition, 2025

**Disclaimer**

This book is intended for informational and inspirational purposes only. The stories, case studies, and individuals referenced throughout are either fictionalized composites or are used with permission. Any resemblance to actual people, living or dead, is purely coincidental and unintentional. These examples are designed to reflect common themes and experiences among neurodivergent individuals.

The contents of this book do not constitute medical, psychological, or legal advice. The author is not a licensed medical or mental health professional, and the material herein should not be used as a substitute for professional consultation, diagnosis, or treatment. Always seek the guidance of a qualified healthcare provider with any questions regarding your physical, emotional, or mental health.

The author and publisher disclaim any liability for loss or damage incurred as a result of the use or application of any content presented in this work.

*Dedication:*

*For the Outliers -
Those who are different by design*

# Contents

**Foreword ix**
**Preface xi**
**Introduction: A Different Rhythm xiii**
**Dedication Letter xvii**

### Part 1: Different by Design

Chapter 1: What Is Important to Neurodivergent People ....... 3
Chapter 2: What Is Not Important to Neurodivergent People ....... 10
Chapter 3: The Challenges are Very Real ....... 16
Chapter 4: Healing and Navigating Professional Help ....... 21

### Part 2: The Gifted and Neurodivergent Intersection

Chapter 5: The Powerful and Fierce Intersection ....... 28
Chapter 6: A Soul in Need of Care ....... 33
Chapter 7: Defining "Care" Beyond Productivity ....... 37
Chapter 8: How to Chase Big Dreams Without Melting Down ....... 41
Chapter 9: The Rhythm of Your Energy is Unique to You ....... 46
Chapter 10: The Sacred Power of Saying No ....... 51
Chapter 11: The Art of Sustainable Contribution ....... 56
Chapter 12: The Necessity of Joy and Play ....... 61
Chapter 13: The Quiet Power of Solitude ....... 66

### Part 3: Understanding the Neurodivergent Soul

Chapter 14: Intricate Minds: Shared Landscape of Giftedness, ADHD, and Autism ....... 73
Chapter 15: Living in a World Not Built for You ....... 78
Chapter 16: Sensory Sensitivity and the Soul ....... 83
Chapter 17: Emotional Depth, Empathy, and Overwhelm ....... 87
Chapter 18: The Myth of Brokenness: Unlearning Internalized Ableism ....... 93

### Part 4: Restoring Your Inner World

Chapter 19: Reclaiming the Self After Trauma ....... 99
Chapter 20: Embracing Rest as Radical Care ....... 103

| | |
|---|---:|
| Chapter 21: Repairing Your Inner Dialogue | 112 |
| Chapter 22: Sensory Sanctuaries: Creating Spaces That Soothe | 116 |
| Chapter 23: The Art of Slowing Down | 122 |
| Chapter 24: Rituals for Regulation | 126 |
| Chapter 25: Creativity as Self-Soothing | 130 |
| Chapter 26: What Resistance Says About Your Needs | 134 |
| Chapter 27: Building a Safe Inner Sanctuary | 138 |

### Part 5: Purpose Without Burnout

| | |
|---|---:|
| Chapter 28: The Pressure to Be Extraordinary | 145 |
| Chapter 29: Rethinking Productivity and Worth | 149 |
| Chapter 30: Navigating Special Interests and Hyperfocus | 154 |
| Chapter 31: How to Chase Big Dreams Without Melting Down | 159 |
| Chapter 32: Success Dysphoria: When Achievement Feels Empty | 163 |
| Chapter 33: Sustainable Purpose: Your Right to a Gentle Life | 167 |

### Part 6: Soul Care as a Lifelong Practice

| | |
|---|---:|
| Chapter 34: Cycles of Energy and Shutdown | 173 |
| Chapter 35: Soul Anchors – Practices that Regulate and Renew | 177 |
| Chapter 36: Redefining Resilience – Healing on Your Own Terms | 181 |
| Chapter 37: Spirituality Beyond Dogma - Reclaiming the Sacred on Your Own Terms | 185 |
| Chapter 38: Rebuilding Trust with Your Nervous System | 192 |
| Chapter 39: Designing a Life That Honors Your Energy | 198 |
| Chapter 40: Choosing a Life You Don't Have to Recover From | 204 |
| Chapter 41: The Sacred Act of Unmasking | 209 |
| Chapter 42: Writing Your Own Definition of Success | 214 |
| Chapter 43: The Practice of Self-Compassion | 223 |
| Chapter 44: Belonging to Yourself | 230 |
| Chapter 45: You Are Doing the Work, Receive the Life You Imagine | 235 |

### Part 7: Navigating Relationships

| | |
|---|---:|
| Chapter 46: Loneliness and the Search for Kindred Spirits | 245 |
| Chapter 47: Boundaries for the Hyper-Empathic Soul | 249 |
| Chapter 48: Finding Your Neurodivergent Community | 255 |

Chapter 49: Love in Translation – Intimacy with a Different Operating
 System 260
Chapter 50: Safety in Neurodivergent Relationships 266

**Conclusion: Coming Home to Yourself 271**
**Acknowledgments 273**
**Love Letters to Your Neurodivergent Soul 275**
**Glossary 283**
**Appendix: A Resource Guide for the Neurodivergent Soul 287**
**Epilogue: A Return to the Self 292**
**About the Author 294**

# Foreword

Are you at a point in your life where it's all becoming so clear - you've never quite fit in, and even more so, you've never felt understood. Maybe you sense that you're different, but not in a way that the world has always embraced?

Have you been shrinking to make others comfortable? Have you been dimming your light? Maybe you even feel drained, and like something is wrong with you.

You're not alone - it's not just you. And there is nothing wrong with you. This book is for you.

In this book, you'll find words and explanations for things you have felt but couldn't describe. You'll find numerous case examples that validate your experience and tools to help you reclaim those beautiful parts of yourself that you felt you needed to hide. Your sensitivities, depth, and knowing are not flaws to be hidden - they are superpowers that the world needs. As Dianne always says, you are here for a mighty purpose!

Dianne knows this path because she's walked it personally. And building on a foundation in Counseling and founding recovery programs, Dianne now serves as an Intuitive Mentor for Visionary Leaders. A globally recognized expert in giftedness and neurodivergence, she has helped countless people reclaim all of who they truly are and reconnect with their visionary nature. One of those people is me.

Dianne helped me get unstuck. She helped me clear "shame and gook," as she says, while moving me forward at the same time. I'm living authentically, whole and unmasked, and standing strong in my gifts that I had allowed others to make me believe were flaws. You can do this, too.

If you are holding this book, you're already further along than you may realize at this moment. You have found a Guide who sees and understands you, and she is holding the flashlight, showing you the way to authenticity and wholeness, your vision, and your mighty purpose.

Let's begin!

*Sara Julian*
Founder/CEO
Ignite Flow, LLC
www.igniteflow.me

## Preface

Books have always been a refuge for me. Long before I had language for what made me different, I found pieces of myself tucked between the pages of others' stories, moments when a stranger's words illuminated something I had only ever felt alone. I also know how rare it is to find a book that speaks to the whole inner landscape of a neurodivergent soul in a world that focuses primarily on the mind and intellect.

So many resources for neurodivergent adults focus on how to cope, how to be more productive, how to mask more effectively, how to force yourself into systems that were never built with your nervous system in mind. These books offer tools, yet often leave behind something essential: the tender, the aching self beneath the strategies, the part of you that simply wants to feel at home in your own skin.

This book was born out of this deep inner ache. It is a quiet rebellion against the idea that your worth is measured by how well you perform in a world that does not know how to hold you. I wrote this book because I needed to read it, and because I have spent years listening to others who are longing for the same kind of care. Your silent pain and inner struggles are not going unnoticed.

What if your life is not something to be fixed, rather it is something to be tended, loved and nurtured? What if the very traits that make you feel out of sync are the ones that hold the keys to your deepest sense of belonging?

This book is about learning how to move with your nature, how to craft a way of being that is both nourishing and sustainable. It is about listening to the wisdom of your sensitivity, your intuition, your intense mind, and heart while remembering that these are not burdens. They are your vital and precious resources, created perfectly for you to fulfill your life's mission and vision. This book is not about pushing through, hacking your brain, or squeezing yourself into someone else's rhythm.

I wrote this book for the ones who feel like they are always trying to keep up in this distracting world. For the ones who live in cycles of burnout and shutdown. For the souls who long to create, to rest, to connect, and have never been shown how to do so in a way that honors the whole being.

This book is for you. It is an invitation to stop trying to become someone else's version of yourself, and instead, to learn how to care for yourself as you are. This book is created to remind you of your inherent value as a human being. It is time to release the identification with human doing and bring forth you as a human being!

With every page, I hope you feel seen. I hope you feel less alone. Most of all, I hope you feel the quiet possibility that there is another way, one where your softness, your slowness, and your different rhythm is a vital asset, not a flaw to overcome or change. Your neurodivergence and giftedness are the very essence of what makes you whole.

I remember the moment when I first realized my exhaustion was not a personal failing, it was my body asking for a different kind of care. I had spent years pushing through, trying to meet the world's demands while ignoring my own inner signals. It was not until I reached the edge of burnout once again, that I finally allowed myself to ask, "What if I can't keep up because I'm not supposed to? What if my intense sensitivity and my different rhythm are not obstacles? What if my rhythm is an invitation into a more aligned way of being?" These questions cracked something open in me, the beginning of unlearning everything I thought I had to be, and listening instead to the yearning of my soul that was quietly asking for a more aligned way of living that was friendly to my nervous system.

This journey is profoundly sacred. It is not always easy. You do not have to walk it alone. This book is designed to inspire and support your life as you allow your innermost vision to emerge.

## INTRODUCTION

# A DIFFERENT RHYTHM

There was a time I thought my soul was broken. In fact, many times throughout my life I wondered about being so depressed then full of energy and creativity that I thought I was an alien somehow. I was clearly not like the others in my family or peer group. I remember thinking while in high school that there was something different about me that I did not understand and people were afraid of me. I have experienced deep grief and many losses because of my neurodivergence that was never acknowledged in a way to help that younger version of me feel seen or understood.

I lived with the quiet ache that something in me would never quite fit, not with the world, not with others, and especially not with the relentless pace of life. My mind raced with too many thoughts, my heart felt too much, and I seemed to need more rest and more space than anyone around me. The very qualities that made me vibrant like my deep empathy, my way of seeing connections others missed, and my hunger for meaning were often the same ones that made life feel unbearably hard. If you are holding this book, perhaps you know this ache too.

The world has plenty of language for what makes us different: Gifted. ADHD. Autistic. Intensely Sensitive. Twice Exceptional (2e). Neurodivergent. These labels can offer clarity, a flicker of relief after years of self-blame and unspeakable grief. They often fail to capture what it feels like to be a soul moving through the world at a different rhythm and with intense sensitivities. The inner experience of living in a body and mind that perceives, processes, and feels everything more is not just a clinical diagnosis. This experience is a different level of consciousness where we feel deeply and perceive what is not known to others. It is a spiritual condition, one that requires a different kind of care.

This book is a guide for tending to your neurodivergent soul. Learning how to truly care for your intensely sensitive, complex, radiant being is essential. I am not referring to merely managing symptoms or chasing productivity. Caring about and for yourself is at the core is vital for your overall health, wellness, and happiness.

I write to you as someone who walks this path, both as an Intuitive Gifted Mentor, Visionary, and as a neurodivergent woman who has spent much of her life searching for meaning and belonging. Over the years, I have worked with gifted adults, creatives, and deep feelers who quietly carry the same questions in their hearts:

- Why do I feel so fragile in a world that seems to expect so much?
- How can I care for my body and mind without betraying my soul?
- What if I never learn how to keep up?
- Is there a way to live that honors my natural rhythm using my differences rather than surviving despite my differences?

These questions have haunted my innermost world for decades. The answers are not always quick or easy. I want you to know there is a way. There is a way to tend to yourself that does not require numbing, shrinking, or forcing yourself to become someone you were never meant to be.

Caring for your neurodivergent soul means to move at the pace of your own being. Listen deeply to what your system needs like rest, beauty, quiet, intensity, or wild bursts of creation. It is time to unlearn the story you were taught that you are fragile or defective. It is time to begin trusting that your rhythm carries its own profound wisdom. Come as you are and experience your life, knowing you are right on time.

This book is more like a lantern, something small and steady to carry with you as you find your own way. It is not a map with fixed destinations as there is no finish line. Think of mile markers or trail markers, guiding your path. This frees you from destination addiction. Each chapter will offer reflections, gentle practices, and soul care rituals to help you tend to your nervous system, reclaim your intense sensitivity, and craft a life that feels both spacious and sustainable.

Wherever you are on your journey, whether you have just begun to name your neurodivergence or have known your whole life, I want you to know that you are not broken, too much, or alone. You are worthy of care, exactly as you are. Allow me to walk with you as you unfold the magic within you.

You will find resonance in the stories, and it is my hope that with each one, you feel seen and valued. Some of the stories are from my own life and some are composites of stories I have witnessed in various forms over my lifetime.

Let us dive into the wonder of your neurodivergence and how to care deeply and authentically for your entire self!

May my words inspire and support you,

*Dianne*

# Dedication Letter

For Dianne,

There are some people whose presence becomes a lifeline before you even realize you're drowning. You have been that for me.

This case study is more than a reflection. It is a constellation of moments, memories, and miracles born from your unwavering faith in who I am, even when I could not see it myself. You have held the light through every threshold, from joy to grief, collapse to rising, and mirrored my brilliance until I had the courage to believe in it.

You have taught me how to nourish my intensities, how to care for the soul behind the genius, and how to lead from the inside out. Because of you, I no longer walk through life wondering if there is something wrong with me. I walk in the truth that I was made this way, and it is beautiful.

Thank you for guiding me home to myself. This is for you, and because of you.

With infinite gratitude and love,

*Michelle*

## Introduction: When Someone Truly Gets You

Sometimes in life, you meet someone who does not just understand what you are saying, they understand *you*. From the inside out. Dianne Allen is that someone for me.

This is the story of how Dianne walked with me from our first meeting in 2002 through decades of transformation. It is about recovering from pathologized intensity. It is about rebuilding a life not *in spite of* neurodivergence, but *because of it*. And it is about the power of mentorship when it's rooted in love, vision, and truth.

**Part One: 2002–2013 - Colleague. Friend. Mirror of Joy.**
"It was like meeting an old friend. I just remember feeling like I had met somebody like me."

In 2002, I walked into Dianne Allen's office for the first time. I had just completed my master's degree in art therapy and have returned from six months of world travel with my fiancé. It was my first week at my first real job out of graduate school, at a substance abuse clinic in Florida and I was eager to make a meaningful contribution.

The environment was heavy. Clients were deep in the struggle with addiction, and the system around us was not built to nurture new ideas. But when I walked into Dianne's office, something changed. She was sitting behind her desk wearing a flowing blue outfit, her eyes glinted with glee and her smile lit up the room. I immediately felt seen. Safe. Energized. Alive.

We clicked instantly. Over the course of our time working there, we realized how much we shared:

- A deep spiritual foundation
- A passion for 12-step recovery and the psychology of transformation
- Athletic discipline and high-performance work ethic
- Intensity: intellectual, emotional, and spiritual

"She was the first person who matched my ability to get to the heart of the matter and also my joy. We did not just see the truth. We believed in transformation."

At the time, I was newly married, struggling with a mysterious autoimmune condition, and standing at a crossroads. Would I stay in the field of therapy? Or move toward something aligned with my visions, creativity, and business desires? No matter my choice, the calling to serve more people in new and different ways was undeniable. Making sure I maintained my health given my high-performance nature, was imperative.

Dianne became a friend and a guide. She introduced me to books on nutrition, movement, ADHD, and emotional wellbeing. I had no language for neurodivergence at that time, but she supported me anyway. She shared my vision to creatively serve and invited me into new roles, including a treatment center that served executives and their families. I followed her lead because I trusted her spirit, her vision, and her integrity.

We both gave everything we had. We worked hard, laughed harder, and began a friendship that would become one of the most anchoring forces in my life.

> "She did not just mentor me, she celebrated me. She mirrored my intensity and helped me begin to believe that maybe, just maybe, I was not broken".

## Part Two: 2013–2023 - From Conversations to Collaborations to Catalysts

"True to our neurodivergent nature, Dianne has played many roles in my life." As the years passed, our friendship deepened. Though our professional lives began to move in different directions, Dianne into coaching and mentoring, and me into creative entrepreneurship and corporate innovation, we never lost connection. We would cross paths at events, share business strategies, and always land in the same kinds of conversations: soul-deep, idea-rich, joyful, and real.

I was consulting around the world. Dianne was expanding her coaching practice to gifted executives in the Americas and Europe. We were visioning. We were building. We were actively turning intensity into innovation.

In 2017 Dianne invited me to visually capture one of her sold out executive coaching workshops. It was a pivotal day. For the first time, I saw the *depth* of the transformational model she had been cultivating. She was not just a coach or a consultant, she was a systems healer. She had developed an intuitive, spiritual, and actionable way to work with high-performing, gifted, emotionally intense, and often pathologized leaders.

"She was not diagnosing or fixing people. She was gathering visionaries and helping them remember their gifts."

That workshop helped me understand how powerful her work truly was, and how aligned it was with mine. We both served brilliant misfits. The "too-much" people. The ones who lived out loud but often suffered quietly. The ones who need a simple shift towards their gifts, and they catapult into building new futures!

That same year, I began to refer my clients to Dianne. One of the first was a business owner with a gifted teen in crisis. We had completed a year of systems optimization, culture building and service design in his company, but his family needed deeper support. When he called and asked me for guidance, I then referred him to Dianne. She worked with them privately and helped them find healing. That young man, once struggling in high school grew into a thriving, purpose-driven leader throughout college and beyond.

Soon after, I recommended to Dianne a family member of my own, someone who had lived under the weight of addiction and misdiagnosis for decades. Through her mentorship, he found long-term sobriety, employment, confidence, and peace. For the first time in his fifty-year life, he felt seen and safe.

"Dianne does not just support the person in front of her. She sees the entire system and works with its energy. That is why the transformation lasts."

We also teamed up on a major neuroscience project with a university researching Alzheimer's prevention. I brought visual innovation and facilitation. Dianne brought deep insight into leadership and vision. Together, we helped craft a granting and growth strategy that empowered researchers to think with more soul and less rigidity.

"It was a neurodivergent playground made in heaven."

During these years, Dianne continued to walk beside me. Our conversations deepened. We talked about patterns. About giftedness. About burnout. She kept repeating something that I still could not quite believe:

"There is nothing wrong with you. You were made this way. And it is beautiful."

It was not until 2024 that those words would land fully. But these were the years she sowed the seeds.

## Part Three: 2024 – The Turning Point: The Collapse, the Awakening, the Rebirth

"I was no longer living in a world of pathology. I was now living in a world of promise."

In early 2024, everything I had been holding together collapsed in a matter of days. A multi-year deception in my family came to light. In just 72 hours, I lost nearly everything: financial security, my business, my home, and a set of relationships I thought would last forever. The emotional and spiritual impact was total.

What made it even more complex was that I did not yet have the language for the magnitude of what was happening. I was only beginning to understand the full legacy of trauma and narcissistic abuse that had shaped my life. The truth emerged fast and hard, and it left no stone unturned.

Dianne was there.

She was the only person who could truly hold it. She had the range, the depth, the tenderness, and the tools. For 45 days straight, she mentored me daily. She helped me stabilize my nervous system using the Safe and Sound Protocol. She reminded me of my rituals. She helped me regulate, rebuild, and finally find rest. She became my lighthouse.

"She held space for the unspeakable without turning away and never once lost sight of my brilliance."

There was no spiritual bypass. No false positivity. Just Presence. Just Truth. And it was in that presence that I began to remember what she had always told me:

"There is nothing wrong with you. You are brilliant. And your gifts are here for others."

Still, I did not fully believe her. Until October 2024.

I had read her book *Someone Gets Me*, a book Dianne wrote a couple of years prior and recommended many times. I took a deep dive and with every page, a lifelong mystery was solved. The intensity I had always tried to shrink. The brilliance I had tried to normalize. The deep emotional and spiritual sensitivities I had been told were "too much"? They were not problems. They were *patterns*. They were *gifts*.

I was neurodivergent. I was gifted. And I had been made this way on purpose. "I am a growing machine," I realized. "That is not a dysfunction. *That is design!*" It was not just a personal insight. It was a soul awakening.

Dianne had known it all along. She had held the blueprint for me while I tried to survive in systems that never fit. And now, I could finally begin to live differently.

**Part Four: From Survivor to Sovereign: Designing a Life Around the Soul's Signature**

"Dianne mirrored my genius until I could see it for myself."

After the collapse, something new began to grow, not from force, but from alignment. For the first time, I started creating a life that was built *for* me, not against me. With Dianne's guidance, I began to develop what I now call my *Personal Operating Manual*, a customized guide for how my neurodivergent, spiritually sensitive, emotionally intense system thrives.

Dianne did not impose a method. She co-created a rhythm. Together, we shaped rituals, structures, reflections, and self-care practices tailored to my gifts. We talked about nervous system regulation, polyvagal theory, creativity cycles, energy windows, and the sacred art of rest. We built in joy. We made it beautiful and livable.

"Working with Dianne is like dancing with who you really are as a cosmic creation."

Through that process, I stopped seeing myself as someone who needed fixing. I started seeing myself as someone who needed framing and feeding. I created systems that honored my imaginative intensity, sensory processing needs, drive for meaning, and need for aesthetic beauty. I stopped trying to squeeze into the neurotypical world and started *designing from my inner cosmos.*

She also helped me connect my spiritual self with my leadership self. No more compartmentalization. I am a mystic and a strategist. I am a healer and a builder. I am emotional and I am executive.

"I am no longer surviving. I am sovereign. And I am shining."

And Dianne? She didn't just cheer me on; she partnered in that unfolding. We "gifted-up" with each other, sharing resources, reflections, breakthroughs, and practices. She even created podcast episodes inspired by our conversations. She trusted my genius and helped me trust it too.

We've created a relationship that is reciprocal, reverent, and radiant. And that's what it means to mentor the neurodivergent soul, not to control it, but to collaborate with it.

Now, I teach others how to build from the inside out. I no longer see myself as someone with too many feelings or ideas. I see myself as someone with a map, and a mission.

## A Sigil, A Symbol, A Shine

If I had to capture everything Dianne has been to me in one image, it would be this:

> A sparkly unicorn, sitting cross-legged in a supernova,
> wearing a crystal diamond mala.
> In one hand, she holds an open journal. In the other, a marker.
> On the left page, there is a heart drawn facing her.
> Because the heart, like her guidance, was never for
> the world first.
> It was for *her*. And through her, it shines for others.

That unicorn is a symbol of what it means to be loved, mentored, and understood at the soul level.

Like the sailboat on the water using the wind to move, I have the structure to sail through life leveraging the invisible winds of my nature. Dianne has given me the tools to live with intensity, not against it. She has helped me see my imagination as an engine, not a liability. She has shown me that emotional depth is not something to recover *from*, it's something to build a life *with*.

And perhaps most importantly, she has taught me this:

"Not only is there nothing wrong with you, there is *everything right* with you, for the world."

Because of her, I now live inside a reality where my neurodivergence is not only nourished, it is celebrated. I have systems. I have beauty. I have joy. I have quiet. And I have power.

"Welcome to nourishing neurodivergence."

I am no longer just a survivor.

I am sovereign.

I am radiant.

I am ready to help others shine too.

*Michelle*

PART 1

# DIFFERENT BY DESIGN

# CHAPTER 1

# WHAT IS IMPORTANT TO NEURODIVERGENT PEOPLE

One of the most liberating truths for the neurodivergent soul is this: you are not failing because something is wrong with you, you're struggling because the world was not designed with your wiring in mind. This shift in understanding is powerful. It moves us from internalized shame and self-doubt to clarity and compassion. We stop asking, *"What's wrong with me?"* and begin asking, *"What do I truly want or need?"*

In my work with gifted and neurodivergent adults, this moment of reframing is often a turning point. When we realize that our difficulties are not personal defects but systemic mismatches, a new world of possibility opens. We begin to shed the exhausting act of constant adaptation and reclaim the authority to define what sustains us. Instead of bending ourselves to meet external standards, we learn to honor our inner compass.

Neurodivergent people tend to orient themselves to the world through five core drivers: Interest, Novelty, Challenge, Urgency, and Passion. These are neurological and emotional necessities instead of frivolous desires or signs of being "distractible" or "too intense." They are how we connect, how we thrive, and how we express our gifts in the world.

Without these elements, life can feel dull, draining, or disorienting.

With them, we experience vitality, focus, and creative flow. Recognizing and cultivating these drivers is not a luxury, it is a form of soul care. These essential needs are the foundation of well-being for many neurodivergent people, and they deserve to be named, protected, and prioritized without apology.

This chapter invites you to explore each of these drivers in depth as living truths that can guide you back to your most aligned and energized self.

**Interest: Your Doorway to Engagement**
Neurodivergent individuals often need genuine interest in a task to fully engage with it. This isn't laziness or lack of willpower, it's neurological. For many with ADHD, autism, or gifted sensitivities, the brain lights up and sustains attention when something is *truly compelling*. But when something feels irrelevant or imposed, engagement feels almost physically impossible.

In my mentoring, I often remind clients: "If you're bored, it doesn't mean you are broken, it might mean you are not being met at your level of depth or curiosity". When interest is sparked, focus sharpens, ideas flow, and energy rises. Interest is the soul's way of saying, "This idea or experience matters to me."

**Novelty: Your Drive to Experience the New**
Many neurodivergent individuals crave newness born from a desire to keep their mind stimulated and their spirit awake. Novelty brings freshness, surprise, and a kind of creative oxygen. In a world that often values predictability and routine, this need can be misunderstood.

Without novelty, you may begin to feel trapped or disengaged. Your environment becomes stale, and your motivation wanes. You are about staying connected to life, not about seeking chaos, even when you may wonder about your life experiences. Novelty, for your neurodivergent soul, can feel like a sacred spark, an invitation to be fully present, to explore, and to feel alive. When your novelty is embraced, whether through learning, experimentation, or change, new pathways open. Novelty can be as simple as taking a different route home, diving into a new subject of study, or rearranging a room.

For gifted and neurodivergent people, your need for novelty is often a spiritual experience: it brings a sense of expansion and possibility. It awakens dormant parts of the self and invites curiosity to lead. You can honor it as an internal compass pointing you toward growth, rather than viewing this drive as distraction or restlessness. In a well-lived life, novelty is essential nourishment for the mind, body, and soul.

**Challenge: Your Call to Grow and Transform**
Contrary to the stereotype of being "unmotivated," many neurodivergent people thrive on complexity. You seek intellectual and emotional challenges because you hunger for depth, not only for competition's sake. You want to grow, to push edges, to wrestle with the big questions that others may shy not yet see or even avoid. This is about becoming yourself rather than about proving yourself.

When placed in environments that are too shallow, rigid, or performative, your inner fire can become dimmed. Monotony and surface-level tasks feel soul-deadening and you may shut down or rebel. When a challenge is aligned with your strengths, values, and interests, you come alive. You are not trying to escape effort; you are trying to escape meaningless effort. Challenge must be paired with purpose to become a catalyst instead of a seeming burden.

In my mentoring work and writing, including *Care for the Neurodivergent Soul*, I often emphasize that neurodivergent brilliance emerges from meaningful engagement. Often, my guidance helps gifted and intensely sensitive adults reframe challenges as a sacred call to evolve, not as a threat to happiness or sanity. I often say, "Your path will likely be nonlinear, yet it is deeply aligned when guided by your inner truth."

When you meet challenges that resonate with your inner world, you do not just rise to the occasion, you transcend your own expectations. Things always work out better than you think. Growth, for your neurodivergent soul, is always wanting to emerge into your life more fully. Growth essentially is always happening because the Universe is always expanding, and you get to choose your level of engagement and willingness to answer your inner longing. This core longing is a call you are born to answer.

**Urgency: Your Power of Now**
Some of us do not truly access our full energy until a deadline looms or the pressure builds. While this can often be misjudged as procrastination, it is often a manifestation of how your neurodivergent brain processes time, motivation, and engagement. Urgency provides clarity and momentum. The stakes help you focus your attention on what matters. Your brain clicks into gear, energy rises, and distractions fall away.

This is not laziness, it is your neurology. Many gifted and neurodivergent individuals experience time blindness, where future events do not register as real until they are emotionally salient or immediate. Your nervous system often needs emotional relevance to activate, and urgency delivers that relevance like a lightning bolt. Urgency pulls scattered energy into a sharp point of action, and this is when you can deliver results unlike many of your counterparts or colleagues.

Living in constant reaction to pressure can be draining. Learning to harness urgency without depending on crisis is a vital practice for you to master. Many of my clients, through mentoring work, learn to create what I call *ethical urgency* which is self-imposed mini-deadlines, accountability rituals, creative sprints, or time-limited containers that generate focus without fueling anxiety or burnout.

In my work with neurodivergent adults, I often help clients transform urgency from a survival pattern into a sustainable strategy. When used with intention, urgency becomes less about panic and more about presence. It becomes a tool for your embodiment, a way of saying, "Now matters, and I choose to show up."

**Passion: Your Flame That Sustains**
Perhaps the most powerful driver of all for you may be your passion. When you care deeply, everything changes. The neurodivergent mind and heart are wired to go all in all the time. Passion ignites your purpose, pulls you through difficulty, and gives you energy even when you're tired. It is the antidote to apathy.

For gifted and neurodivergent individuals, passion is a necessity, not just a good idea. Passion offers a sense of orientation in a world that can feel chaotic, numbing, or overwhelming. Passion is how you connect to meaning. It is the inner fire that says, "This is worth my energy. This is why I am here." You may become deeply absorbed, even obsessive, when something captures your interest, not because you lack self-control, but because your entire system is activated in the presence of true engagement.

The problem is, our culture often asks you to suppress passion in the name of "balance," "professionalism," or conformity. This dimming of your intense sensitivities can lead to disengagement, depression, or a sense of being lost. In my mentoring work with gifted people like you, I have seen time and again: passion is your lifeblood not a liability like many people I know have been bullied about or taught. When you follow what lights you up, you do not burn out, you burn bright.

As I often tell clients, "You were never too much. You were simply misread in a world that forgot how to honor deep devotion." When your passion is channeled wisely, it fuels sustainable creativity, authentic leadership, and profound personal evolution. Passion is what sustains you when nothing else makes sense. It is the core of your alignment. You thrive not by extinguishing your fire, but by giving it room to breathe. Fan your flames!

**Meet Daniel**
Daniel is a 40-year-old software developer and father of two who came into mentoring depleted and disheartened. Though highly

skilled and respected, he confessed, *"I'm so checked out. I stare at code all day, and nothing lights me up anymore."* He had been in the same role for seven years, and despite promotions, he felt disengaged and restless. His work was no longer feeding his soul.

In our sessions, it became clear Daniel had been starving for challenge and novelty. He was no longer learning, no longer stretching. His natural curiosity had atrophied under the weight of routine. We explored what had previously sparked him and uncovered an early love of creative problem solving and building systems from scratch. Daniel, as he rediscovered, is insanely creative and loves the creative process including solving complex problems.

Over the next few months, Daniel began to reclaim his interest and passion in creativity and problem solving. He started an open-source side project that involved designing software for neurodivergent-friendly scheduling apps, an idea born out of his own journey. This project hit every core value: it was urgent, meaningful, novel, and deeply personal.

Daniel shared, *"I feel alive again. I forgot what it was like to be excited about something."* With renewed energy, he brought more innovation into his day job and began advocating for more flexible structures at work. Daniel had realigned his life around what truly mattered to his neurodivergent brain and his soul.

After 3 months, Daniel reported that "My family is happier too, because I am less grouchy and not so frustrated. I am a better person now because my inner self is satisfied." Daniel continues to create and fulfill his work responsibilities and now he has the support and encouragement of his co-workers and family.

**Reflection Questions**

1. When in your life have you felt most engaged or lit up? What elements were present, interest, novelty, challenge, urgency, or passion?

2. Which of these five drivers is most active in your life right now? Which one is missing or suppressed?

3. How has your need for interest or passion been misunderstood or mischaracterized in school, work, or relationships?

4. What new structures or habits could you experiment with that honor your natural motivation patterns?

5. If you gave yourself full permission to follow what fascinates you without guilt, what would change in your daily life?

## CHAPTER 2

# WHAT IS NOT IMPORTANT TO NEURODIVERGENT PEOPLE

Certain motivators simply do not register for your neurodivergent mind. They do not land, do not inspire, and often cause more harm than good. These are the very motivators society leans on to enforce compliance: fear, boredom, shame, superficial praise, and rigid consequences. Designed to maintain order, these tools frequently erode trust and extinguish curiosity in those of us who are wired for depth, sensitivity, and meaning.

When educators, employers, or caregivers insist that these methods *should* work, they often miss something fundamental. Your neurodivergent nervous system responds to connection not to control. What looks like resistance is often misalignment. What looks like defiance is often neurological dissonance. Ignoring this gap creates not just missed opportunities, but layers of shame, mislabeling, and unnecessary struggle for all concerned.

When you are saying, *"I just can't get started,"* it is rarely about laziness. In my mentoring practice, I've learned to listen beneath those words to what is not being said. What often sounds like a lack of motivation is actually a tangle of invisible barriers such as burnout, overwhelm, emotional dysregulation, decision fatigue, sensory overload, compassion fatigue, or a lack of meaningful connection to the task at hand.

Motivation for your neurodivergent soul is sparked by resonance. It requires relevance, emotional safety, congruence, and a sense of internal alignment. Without these elements, even the most capable and passionate person may freeze. Not because they don't care, but because you care so much, and cannot find the bridge from vision to action.

Too many gifted individuals have internalized the belief that their inconsistent energy means they are unreliable or broken. This cannot be further from the truth. In reality, you are navigating a nervous system that processes the world differently, most often more deeply, more intensely, more personally. Your unique difference requires enhanced attunement instead of judgment.

As a mentor, I guide clients back to their own inner compass. We inquire. We listen to what any resistance is trying to say. We don't push through blocks. We ask instead, *"Is it fear? Is it fatigue? Is it a signal that the task is misaligned with your values?"*. Often, the motivation returns because we got honest and were willing to take focused action both in mindset, words and behaviors. Working together yields powerful results for the neurodivergent people with whom I have the honor of mentoring.

Honoring your energy is powerful wisdom, not indulgence like so many may believe. This is the foundation for sustainable motivation, creative momentum, and meaningful contribution for you and other gifted people. When you create from alignment instead of expectation, you don't need to force motivation, it flows through you with ease and grace.

## Consequences: The Broken Motivator

Traditional behavior systems rely on consequences, detentions, reprimands, performance reviews, demotions, the constant weighing of outcomes. These systems assume that future discomfort or reward will shape present behavior. For many neurodivergent people, this logic fails completely. You have most likely run headfirst into these types of scenarios in your life.

Executive functioning differences can distort your time perception. The distance between action and outcome often feels like a void instead of a bridge. Saying "you'll regret this later" to someone with ADHD or trauma-related processing challenges is like whispering across a canyon that nothing makes it to the other side. There is a difference in your internal wiring and processing. This is not a failure of discipline. The result? Confusion, self-blame, and a growing chasm between intention and action.

You, as a neurodivergent person, may know what's expected and still be unable to act in alignment. Shame can build up when you are told you "Should have known better." In truth, you are often operating without access to the tools others take for granted. Once you are able to honor your neurodivergent ways, you will connect with your authentic motivators.

What supports change is present-moment engagement, something that feels real right now. Relevance, emotion, and personal connection are powerful bridges that help you reengage your motivator. When tasks are tied to your identity, purpose, or contribution, internal motivation awakens. When guidance speaks to your nervous system in language you can feel things begin to shift and your inner world and outer actions align and work together much more effectively.

**Boring Activities: The Motivation Killer**

Monotony drains your neurodivergent mind like a slow leak. Repetition without purpose is intolerable. Mundane tasks can feel physically painful agitating, numbing, or disorienting. It is a mismatch in cognitive your need in relation to your external environment. It is not about your preference or your internal environment.

Rigid systems built on repetition and routine expect neurodivergent people to comply without engagement. That compliance comes at a cost that includes emotional exhaustion, nervous system overload, or outright shutdown. Without meaningful stimulation, even the simplest task becomes insurmountable. I am sure you have felt this at some point in your life. You may even be feeling this now.

This is not you being lazy. This is your brain that needs stimulation to sustain focus trying to get your attention. Your nervous system searches for novelty, depth, movement, or beauty to feel alive. When nothing engages your soul, everything becomes overwhelming. This is when you eventually shut down or break down.

There are creative ways to respond. Movement, music, sensory enrichment, co-working, and reframing tasks through meaning or contribution can make a profound difference. Some people delegate while others use timers or create rituals of celebration. The key is this: boredom is a signal that something vital is missing, not a minor inconvenience.

**Empty Praise and External Rewards: The Echo Chamber**
Authenticity matters more than approval. You, as a neurodivergent person, often feel the dissonance between what is said and what you feel. When praise is shallow, it echoes without resonance. When rewards are offered without meaning, they feel more like manipulation than motivation. Gold stars, employee-of-the-month awards, or hollow affirmations rarely move someone who sees through surface performances. These tools assume that the appearance of success is enough. It is not.

Many gifted and neurodivergent individuals crave feedback that reflects their essence, not merely their output. They want their effort to be witnessed, their process to be understood, their soul to be recognized not just their performance evaluated. Inauthentic praise can breed alienation.

True affirmation, however grounded, specific, attuned can inspire real momentum. When someone says, "I see how deeply you care," or "I noticed the nuance in how you handled that," it creates resonance. Real motivation rises from being seen clearly.

You do not need to work harder to gain louder applause. You need and deserve mirrors that reflect who you really are. For you, being seen and having an understanding of your neurodivergence is paramount.

**Meet Penny**
Penny is a 29-year-old musician and former honors student who came into mentoring sessions riddled with self-doubt. She once told me, "I've always been great at deadlines, but only when I was terrified. Now that I work for myself, I just... can't move." She was struggling to complete her album, despite having talent and time.

In our early sessions, we traced the problem to her history: Penny had grown up motivated by consequences, grades, guilt, parental pressure. Once those were removed, she felt like she lost her structure. But as we explored deeper, it became clear that the issue wasn't laziness, it was a lack of emotional connection to the work. Her music had become a task, not a passion.

We resurrected her relationship with her art. I introduced a technique I use often: "emotional anchoring." We connected each track she was recording to a meaningful experience or value. She created a studio ritual that included sensory grounding, lighting candles, and reconnecting to why the music mattered.

Instead of forcing productivity through fear, Penny began to create from a place of inner urgency. "I didn't need a deadline," she told me after a few months. "I needed to remember why I started singing in the first place."

Today, she structures her creative time around inspiration instead of something punitive. She has released her first EP and done so without burnout or shame.

**Reflection Questions**

1. When have you felt pressured by consequences that didn't really motivate or inspire you? How did your body respond?

2. What kinds of tasks or routines feel lifeless or draining to you, even if they seem "easy" to others? Why do you think that is?

3. Can you recall a time when you were praised or rewarded but still felt unseen or unmotivated? What would authentic recognition have looked like?

4. What systems in your life currently rely on motivation methods that don't actually work for you? What could shift?

5. What internal values or emotional connections help you stay motivated without needing fear or external pressure? How can you nurture those more regularly?

## CHAPTER 3

# THE CHALLENGES ARE VERY REAL

To be gifted and neurodivergent is to experience the world through a heightened lens: brilliant, complex, deeply attuned, and often profoundly overwhelming. This unique wiring brings immense gifts: insight that sees beneath the surface, intuition that senses what others miss, creativity that reimagines what's possible. But alongside these strengths come equally intense challenges, challenges that are frequently minimized, misinterpreted, or pathologized by systems that weren't built with this wiring in mind.

Many gifted and neurodivergent individuals struggle because they are navigating environments that demand linear thinking, social conformity, and emotional suppression. Sensory overload in chaotic spaces, transitions without warning, emotionally shallow interactions, and rigid routines can all create invisible barriers to your thriving. The world often rewards compliance over curiosity, speed over depth, and consistency over innovation leaving you exhausted from masking, shame, self-doubt, or trying to "fit in."

These difficulties are signs of a mismatch. You are not failing even though you may feel that way at times. Understanding these friction points whether they show up in school, work, relationships, or daily life can help you reclaim your power. When you recognize that the challenge lies not within you but in the context, you can approach life with more compassion, strategy, and self-trust. Being different means learning to thrive on your own terms. You are not broken.

**Transitions: The Invisible Earthquakes**
For many neurodivergent individuals, transitions are far more than logistical shifts, they are *energetic ruptures*. Moving from one activity to another, even when both are enjoyable, can trigger a stress response. Ending something that offers structure, starting something unknown, or switching mental gears without adequate processing time can feel physically jarring.

Transitions often activate your sensory, emotional, and executive functioning systems all at once. Your nervous system is asked to release one focus and orient to another, sometimes with no time to recalibrate. This can result in irritability, shutdown, or confusion, especially in fast-paced environments that expect instant pivoting.

In mentoring, I often teach that *transitions need to be honored like ceremonies*. Rituals, buffer zones, music, or breathwork can help soften the shift and signal safety. For your neurodivergent soul, transitions are not just tasks, they are thresholds or bridges.

**Workplace Social Norms: The Unspoken Maze**
Neurodivergent people often struggle not with the *work* itself, but with the social undercurrents of professional settings. Office politics, passive communication, and unspoken expectations can feel like you are in a maze with no map.

You may feel frustrated by inefficiency or meaningless protocols. Autistic or intensely sensitive people may find small talk exhausting or confusing. For many, masking becomes a daily survival strategy, exhausting, depleting, and alienating themselves from self and others.

These social norms often prioritize your assimilation over your authenticity. In my mentoring work, I encourage clients to find *micro-honest ways to be themselves*, from opting out of nonessential social events to creating collaborative relationships rooted in clarity and respect. Workplace success for neurodivergent adults doesn't require conformity, it requires courage, and often, creative boundary-setting while navigating the often-confusing landscape of expectations.

**Repetitive Tasks Without Meaning: Cognitive Sandpaper**
Tasks that are repetitive, shallow, or disconnected from interest can feel unbearable for gifted and neurodivergent minds. While many systems assume everyone can "just do the boring stuff," this overlooks a key neurological reality: without meaning or stimulation, the neurodivergent brain shuts down, gets distracted, or goes into avoidance.

This isn't a mindset issue. It's a mismatch of cognitive fuel. Without novelty, challenge, or emotional relevance, energy drops out. Many clients describe these tasks as "cognitive sandpaper", irritating, numbing, and overwhelming all at once.

In mentoring, I often help clients reframe or restructure these tasks: pairing them with movement, batching them into short sprints, or outsourcing them entirely when possible. The key is recognizing that your resistance to repetition is not laziness, it is your unique wiring, and you deserve solutions that work with your brain.

**Meet Simone**
Simone is a 35-year-old architect and gifted visual thinker who came into mentoring in a state of deep fatigue. She described a cycle of high performance followed by burnout, especially during workdays filled with back-to-back meetings, deadline pivots, and constant switching between design tasks and team management.

"I feel like I'm constantly changing masks," she said. "By the end of the day, I can't remember who I am or what I even care about."

As we worked together, it became clear that Simone's exhaustion was rooted in two main challenges: relentless transitions and workplace social norms that demanded constant adaptability and people-pleasing. She was navigating a workplace that rewarded charm and flexibility but punished pause, slowness, or silence.

We co-created a strategy that honored her needs. She began

building intentional transition time into her calendar, even five minutes between meetings to breathe, stretch, or listen to grounding music made a difference. She implemented a "soft close" at the end of each workday to recalibrate and reorient to herself.

We also developed scripts for professional self-advocacy, helping Simone reduce unnecessary social labor and delegate repetitive admin tasks. With time, she began feeling more energized, less resentful, and more in tune with her own rhythms.

Simone shared, "I used to think I was just bad at life. Now I realize I was trying to live someone else's version of it."

## Reflection Questions

1. Which kinds of transitions (daily, seasonal, relational, or career-related) feel most destabilizing to you? What helps you move through them with grace?

2. How have unspoken social rules or workplace expectations challenged your authenticity or drained your energy?

3. Are there any repetitive tasks in your life that feel especially exhausting? How might you reframe, restructure, or delegate them to reduce friction?

4. What hidden rules or norms have you been following just to "get by"? What would it feel like to begin living by your own rules and norms?

5. If you treated your difficulties not as deficits but as invitations for new strategies, what would change in your self-talk and daily habits?

CHAPTER 4

# HEALING AND NAVIGATING PROFESSIONAL HELP

Healing is rarely linear, especially for neurodivergent individuals who carry layered experiences of trauma, chronic stress, health challenges, or addiction. The path forward often requires tending to multiple layers at once, the body, the mind, the nervous system, and the soul. For many, healing means facing not only internal wounds but also navigating systems that misunderstand or mislabel them. Recovery and repair are not isolated events; they are intertwined journeys that demand compassion, strategy, and support. In this chapter, we explore what it means to heal on multiple fronts, how to reclaim agency in your recovery, advocate for your needs in medical and therapeutic settings, and build a care ecosystem that honors your unique neurodivergent rhythm.

**The Overlapping Terrain of Healing**
For many neurodivergent individuals, healing is not linear, and it is rarely singular. The path to wellness often involves navigating recovery from substance use, managing chronic physical or mental health conditions, and engaging with systems of care that were not designed with neurodivergent wiring in mind.

Whether you are walking the path of recovery from addictive behaviors, managing autoimmune illness, or seeking mental health support, your neurodivergent traits, your intensity, sensory sensitivity, or communication style can influence every interaction and outcome. These overlapping journeys can feel like an intricate dance with multiple tempos and unfamiliar steps.

In a world built for conformity, neurodivergent people are often misread, misdiagnosed, or underserved in medical and therapeutic settings. Substance use can arise not from recklessness but from attempts to numb sensory overload, mask emotional intensity, or cope with a life that never seemed to fit. Chronic health challenges may go unrecognized for years, dismissed as anxiety or somatic complaints, when in truth the body is crying out for regulation, care, and safety.

**Addiction and Recovery Through a Neurodivergent Lens**
This section explores the nuances of being neurodivergent and in recovery whether from substances, trauma, or health crises and how to approach helping professionals with your whole self-intact. Substance use in neurodivergent adults is often misunderstood. What might be seen as "self-medicating" can be a way of surviving a system that never met your needs. Gifted and autistic adults may turn to substances to quiet a mind that never stops, or to blunt the pain of social rejection, chronic misunderstanding, or emotional intensity.

Traditional recovery models may not always resonate. For example:
- Group sharing settings may be overwhelming.
- "Higher Power" language may feel alienating or confusing.
- Black-and-white thinking in some 12-step interpretations may clash with a more nuanced neurodivergent experience.

Recovery is possible and deeply transformative when it honors your unique needs. Recovery spaces that emphasize self-agency, creative coping, somatic awareness, and gentle pacing are often more successful for neurodivergent individuals.

**Living with Chronic Health Challenges**
Health issues such as autoimmune conditions, chronic fatigue, gastrointestinal disorders, or even long-term mental health conditions can frequently co-occur with neurodivergence. Autistic adults, in particular, have higher rates of co-occurring physical conditions, yet they often experience medical gaslighting.
You may be told:
- "You're just anxious."
- "Your labs are normal."
- "Maybe you're overreacting."

This can lead to deep self-doubt and avoidance of care. Trust your body because it knows. Learning to trust your internal signals again, and advocating for yourself in medical settings, becomes both spiritual and practical practice. Afterall, you know your body better than anyone else. Trust this truth.

**How to Speak to Helping Professionals**
Navigating the care systems: therapists, doctors, case workers, support groups require advocacy, but also strategy. Here are some essential approaches:

**1. Lead with your truth.**
Start by stating: "I'm neurodivergent, and this affects how I process information, feel emotions, and experience my body. I want to collaborate with you, and I may need different approaches or pacing."

**2. Ask for sensory and processing accommodations.**
- Request clear, direct communication.
- Ask for written follow-ups.
- Let them know if fluorescent lights, fast speech, or touch-based exams are difficult.

**3. Clarify your needs.**
You don't need to explain everything, only what's relevant. You may want to overshare in an effort to be heard, or you may struggle with how to say something. Practice being clear prior to any office visit.

For instance:

"I sometimes need time to process before answering." "I tend to mask, so I might not show pain or distress the way you expect."

**4. Bring written notes.**
Write your symptoms, experiences, or questions beforehand. This can help keep you grounded and ensure you're heard. Often, keeping a log or journal of symptoms, experiences, feelings or pains will be helpful. It is easy to forget something important when in an office setting, especially if you are nervous.

**5. Know you can say no.**
You have the right to decline treatment or any recommendation. You have the right to ask for a second opinion, or to request a different provider if you feel unsafe or unseen.

**Meet Devon**
Devon is a 39-year-old gifted adult with ADHD and sensory processing sensitivity who spent years numbing with alcohol. It started in college, where he used drinking to slow his racing thoughts and cope with social anxiety. By the time he sought help, he had also developed autoimmune thyroid disease and struggled with fatigue and gut issues that were constantly dismissed as "just stress."

In therapy and medical settings, Devon masked heavily smiling, making jokes, and downplaying his suffering. He was often labeled "high functioning" and told he didn't "seem like someone with a problem."

It wasn't until he met a somatic recovery coach who recognized his intensity as giftedness and not pathology that Devon began to unmask. He created a new framework for sobriety centered on self-compassion, movement, solitude, and art. He also started working with a neurodivergent-informed doctor who validated his physical symptoms and helped him design a sustainable wellness plan.

Today, Devon sees his recovery not as fixing what's broken, but as reclaiming his nervous system and creative spirit.

Healing for the neurodivergent soul is never just about symptoms or diagnosis; it is about reweaving wholeness from complexity. As we deepen into this journey, we begin to redefine what care means on our terms.

## Reflection Questions

1. What assumptions about recovery or wellness have you internalized that may not fit your neurodivergent reality?

2. Have you ever felt dismissed or misunderstood in a medical or recovery space? What did you need instead?

3. What tools or practices help you feel safe and regulated in your healing journey?

4. How do you advocate for your sensory, communication, or pacing needs with professionals?

5. What would a truly supportive recovery or wellness space look and feel like for you?

PART 2

# THE GIFTED AND NEURODIVERGENT INTERSECTION

# CHAPTER 5

# THE POWERFUL AND FIERCE INTERSECTION

The meeting place between giftedness and neurodivergence is often overlooked, misdiagnosed, or misunderstood. Yet it is precisely in this rich and complex intersection where profound creativity, insight, and intensity reside. While society tends to silo giftedness apart from neurodivergent conditions like ADHD, autism, or sensory processing sensitivity, the lived experience tells a different story. The boundaries are not rigid, they are fluid, overlapping, and nuanced. Many individuals embody both, and in doing so, they carry a unique combination of potential and vulnerability, brilliance and burnout, depth and disorientation.

You may have been thinking or feeling that you have more than one facet of giftedness or neurodivergence. Chances are that you have a flavor or blending of different aspects of neurodivergence and giftedness. The lines are not clear cut. I believe that your lived experience ought to be validated as real.

**The Intersection Is Real**
Giftedness is not just about high IQ or academic acceleration. As I emphasize in my mentoring and teaching, giftedness is a way of being, a life characterized by heightened perception, deep emotional resonance, rapid mental processing, and a relentless hunger for authenticity, meaning, and justice. When that gifted essence is paired with neurodivergence, whether it appears through sensory sensitivities,

social communication differences, nonlinear problem-solving, or executive functioning challenges, the result is a layered, often intense experience of the world.

This dual wiring can lead to extraordinary insight, visionary thinking, and deep empathy, but it can also create a painful mismatch with conventional systems. In most institutions, educational, medical, and social giftedness and neurodivergence are treated as mutually exclusive categories. Gifted students are tracked into enrichment programs; neurodivergent individuals are funneled into therapy or remediation. Those who live at the intersection, the twice exceptional (2e), often fall through the cracks, misread by teachers, misunderstood by peers, and underserved by both paradigms.

This disconnection breeds confusion and invisibility. Many gifted neurodivergent adults grow up feeling too much, too fast, or too complex for the environments around them. You are celebrated for your abilities and pathologized for your differences, praised one moment, shamed the next. The emotional toll of being both gifted and neurodivergent without support or recognition can result in chronic self-doubt, anxiety, masking, and internalized shame.

Yet when this intersection is named, honored, and supported with nuance and compassion, it becomes a wellspring of extraordinary contribution. The task is to understand the dynamic interplay and cultivate spaces where the whole person (you) can be seen, supported, and empowered to thrive. Splitting giftedness from neurodivergence can bring about confusion so I would trust your lived experience.

## Meet Jasmine

Jasmine is a 17-year-old high school student who is profoundly gifted with intense sensitivities, and neurodivergent. Truly, Jasmines' life has many nuances and complexities.

From an early age, Jasmine showed signs of exceptional verbal ability and abstract reasoning. She taught herself to read at three, wrote poetry at six, and could hold philosophical conversations by nine. But her life has not been easy. Jasmine also experiences overwhelming sensory input, fluorescent lights give her headaches, certain fabrics make her skin feel like it's burning, and loud environments cause her to shut down. She's been diagnosed with ADHD and Sensory Processing Disorder. Some therapists suspected autism, though her high masking abilities made it difficult to assess.

Jasmine often felt "too much" for people around her. Teachers praised her intelligence but became frustrated with her lack of organization and emotional intensity. Friends admired her creativity but struggled to understand her need for solitude after social events. Her inner world was rich, but her outer experience was often fraught with misunderstandings.

Her parents tried to support her, but systems kept pushing them to choose: "Is she gifted, or does she need intervention?" Jasmine was both, and neither system alone could hold her full experience.

Eventually, Jasmine's mother (Ruth) contacted me, and we began to unpack Jasmines' situation, challenges and successes. Ruth shared that she had heard of my work with gifted individuals, especially those with intense sensitivities, emphasizing that many challenges of giftedness often come with multipotentiality, emotional intensity, and spiritual depth. Ruth also shared that both she and Jasmine have read my book *Someone Gets Me* and regularly listen to the *Someone Gets Me* podcast. They both had an idea that Jasmine and her family could see her situation with empowerment rather than as a problem to be solved. I reframed Jasmines' intense sensitivities and neurodivergence not as dysfunctions, but as sacred signs of something very unique and special. Jasmine wasn't broken, rather she was wired differently, different by design. Her sensitivity to light wasn't a disorder; it was part of how her body and mind more finely perceived the world. Her emotional depth wasn't overreaction, instead it was an empathic radar picking up what others missed in many situations.

With this lens, Jasmine began to understand that her experiences weren't just symptoms, they were indicators of a unique inner architecture. Instead of trying to suppress her intense sensitivities, she learned to work with them in a productive and empowering way.

Instead of shaming herself for needing alone time, she began to see solitude as a form of energetic regulation. Instead of trying to force herself into neurotypical productivity systems, we co-created methods that honored her natural rhythms.

The result continues to unfold. Jasmine began to thrive, not by becoming "less intensely sensitive and denying her neurodivergence," but by recognizing her intense sensitivities as superpowers.

What Jasmine's story shows is that the gifted and neurodivergent intersection is the sacred calling. Often the artists, healers, inventors, and truth-tellers of the world are similar to Jasmine in many ways. You may feel deeply, see widely, and dream radically. You need a different kind of care, one that affirms your wiring, supports their nervous system, and respects your depth.

To care for the neurodivergent soul at this intersection is to:
- Normalize emotional and sensory intensity
- Create space for non-linear thinking and expression
- Celebrate deep empathy and spiritual connection
- Provide unstructured time for integration and rest
- Allow the individual to define success on their own terms

**Reflection Questions**

1. Where in your life have you felt both gifted and misunderstood? Consider how your intellectual, emotional, or creative intensity may have been mislabeled, ignored, or mistaken for something else.

2. What aspects of your experience don't fit neatly into categories? Reflect on the blend of traits, strengths, sensitivities, and challenges that feel uniquely yours but are often overlooked by traditional definitions.

3. In what ways has the intersection of giftedness and neurodivergence shaped your identity or relationships? Think about how this blending has influenced the way you show up in the world, connect with others, or view yourself.

4. How do you navigate environments that expect you to choose one narrative, gifted or struggling, rather than embracing both? Reflect on how this tension has affected your confidence, your voice, or your ability to advocate for your needs.

5. What kind of validation or acknowledgment do you most need right now? Let yourself name what you would feel truly supportive and honoring of your lived experience at this complex and beautiful intersection.

# CHAPTER 6

# A SOUL IN NEED OF CARE

You are not a problem to be solved. You are a soul to be cared for. There comes a time in the life of every neurodivergent soul when the burden of navigating a world not made for them becomes too great to carry alone. In these moments, exhaustion seeps deeper than the body. It touches the marrow. It quiets the spirit. It reaches the soul.

The constant adaptation, the internal gymnastics required just to be perceived as "functional," wear away at the inner landscape until there is barely enough energy to keep up appearances. The cost of hiding, contorting, translating oneself into palatable fragments, becomes unbearable. This is not a failure. This is a sacred threshold.

True healing begins the moment the soul whispers, "I cannot keep living like this". That whisper, often ignored or delayed, is not a sign of weakness, it is the voice of wisdom. It is the moment of remembering that you are worthy of care that fits you, not care that reshapes you to fit in. Many gifted, ADHD, and autistic adults live with a backlog of invisible injuries. The trauma of being misunderstood. The confusion of intuitive knowing dismissed as overreaction. The ache of relationships that fail to mirror their depth. These wounds accumulate, not always as dramatic events, but as slow erosions of trust and belonging.

Often, the very traits that make them exceptional also isolate them. Their brilliance is noticed, but only when it's useful. Their struggles are overlooked, or pathologized. This fragmentation breeds self-doubt, the kind that hides behind overachievement or people-pleasing, the kind that keeps joy at arm's length.

The truth is: there is nothing wrong with you. There never was. The systems were not built with your rhythm in mind. The support you needed wasn't missing because you were unworthy. It was missing because the world hasn't learned to speak your language.

Soul-centered mentoring has become a lifeline here. It is not performance coaching. It is not fixing. It is a sacred relationship rooted in witnessing, reflecting, and restoring your sense of wholeness. It creates space for you to show up unmasked and unedited. It allows you to re-inhabit your body, your truth, and your original knowing.

This kind of care honors your intensity, your sensitivity, your insight. It meets you where logic ends and soul begins. It invites all your parts, grieving, brilliant, burnt out, visionary back to the table. It makes room for your needs without shame. It helps you rewrite the inner narrative from *"What is wrong with me?"* to *"How can I honor who I am?"*

You are here to be held, understood, and supported in your own language. You are here to return to yourself. You are not here to perform your way into worthiness. You are not here to carry everyone else's expectations on your shoulders.

Let this be the season where your care becomes sacred. Let this be the chapter where your soul is met with tenderness, not tools. Let this be the moment you stop surviving the world and begin creating one that reflects who you truly are.

## Meet Peter

Peter is a 32-year-old gifted adult with twice-exceptionality (giftedness and ADHD) who found himself at a breaking point. On the surface, he was successful: a respected software engineer, a creative thinker admired by his peers. Privately, he struggled with severe burnout, emotional overwhelm, and a persistent sense of not belonging anywhere, not at work, not in friendships, not even within himself.

After several months of escalating anxiety and sleepless nights, Peter reached out for mentoring because traditional therapy has not worked in the past. In his first meeting, he broke down in tears within minutes, apologizing profusely for being "too much."

I listened deeply, creating a sacred space without judgment or rush. I recognized the signs of a soul crying out for care, the weariness behind Peter's brilliant mind, the self-doubt woven into his ambitious goals, the tender heart beneath layers of competence.

Rather than immediately strategizing "solutions," I invited Peter into a different kind of conversation, one that honored his inner world first.

Over several months, our work together focused on restoring Peter's connection to himself:

- **Naming the soul's fatigue**: Peter learned to validate the real nature of his exhaustion instead of dismissing it as weakness.
- **Reframing his sensitivity**: Rather than seeing his emotional depth and sensory sensitivities as liabilities, he began to recognize them as sacred gifts.
- **Building sustainable rhythms**: Together, we designed daily practices to support his nervous system, honor his passions, and set compassionate healthy boundaries.

As Peter reclaimed pieces of himself long buried under performance and perfectionism, he began to experience glimpses of joy again, not the "high" that can come with accomplishment, but the quiet, steady joy of simply being.

Our mentoring work was not about "fixing" Peter; it was about witnessing, guiding, and affirming the wisdom already within him. Healing, as I often remind my mentees, is about coming home to who you have always been, not about becoming someone new.

**Reflection Questions**

1. In what ways have you (or someone you care for) experienced both giftedness and neurodivergence as sources of both challenge and strength?

2. How do your sensitivities show up in daily life emotionally, physically, or spiritually and what would it look like to honor them instead of suppressing them?

3. What systems or narratives in your life have asked you to "choose a side" gifted *or* neurodivergent and how might embracing both create a more whole, authentic path forward?

4. When was the last time you allowed yourself to admit that you needed care, without judgment? In what ways have you been taught to overlook or minimize your inner exhaustion?

5. What would it feel like to offer yourself the same compassion you give to others?

CHAPTER 7

# DEFINING "CARE" BEYOND PRODUCTIVITY

You have been conditioned, perhaps your entire life, to believe that your worth is something to be proven. The world around you, with its obsession for metrics and measurable success, has offered one message again and again: *What you do is more important than who you are.*

As a neurodivergent soul, you may have absorbed this message deeply. Your gifts were praised only when they showed up as achievements. You were celebrated for your test scores, your talents, your ability to outpace your peers, not for your quiet wisdom, your inner world, or your unique way of moving through life. Slowly, and without realizing it, you may have come to equate care with improvement. Rest became something to earn. Joy had to serve a purpose. Even healing felt like a race to get back to "normal."

This transactional way of living disconnects you from your essence. When care is always linked to performance, your nervous system never fully settles. You remain in a loop of doing, fixing, proving—always striving, never arriving. It's time to unhook from that narrative.

Care, real care, is not a productivity hack. It does not ask you to be useful. It does not measure your value in output. Instead, it asks you to soften and to go within and listen. It is inviting you to attend to your needs because they matter, not because they make you more efficient.

When you allow yourself to rest simply because you're tired, that is care. When you pursue something delightful with no agenda, that is care. When you say no, take up space, or slow down even when others keep going, you are honoring the deeper truth of your nervous system, your body, your spirit.

This form of care may feel unfamiliar at first. It may even feel wrong or indulgent. That is the old programming talking, the one that taught you from an early age that love must be earned, that you must always justify your needs, that your softness is a liability. That voice is not your truth. Your truth is this: *You are not a machine. You are a living, breathing soul with rhythms and seasons of your own.*

Let yourself experiment with what care looks like outside of performance. Maybe it's taking a nap without guilt. Maybe it's spending an hour doing something just because it brings you joy. Maybe it's sitting in silence, letting your body catch up with your mind. You get to choose. You get to redefine.

Care is not a reward for pushing through. It is a foundation for thriving. It is how you return to yourself after the world tries to pull you apart. It is how you repair the breach between your worth and your being.

So today, begin where you are. Let your care be slow. Let it be soulful. Let it be enough. You do not have to earn your right to exist gently in this world. You already belong here.

### Meet Isabel

Isabel is a 48-year-old autistic and profoundly gifted artist who came to me after a serious creative block left her feeling disconnected and lost. A well-known figure in her field, she was celebrated for her innovation and prolific output. But privately, Isabel felt numb. Her mind raced constantly, yet her body felt heavy and resistant. "Even when I'm not working," she said, "I feel guilty for resting. Like I'm wasting time if I'm not producing something."

Together, we explored her lifelong pattern of masking her true needs. Growing up, her intense focus and abilities were praised only when they resulted in something measurable. Silence, solitude, or slowness were seen as laziness or eccentricity. Over time, Isabel had internalized a belief that her value was tied solely to what she could deliver fast.

Rather than forcing her back into creative productivity, I invited her to unhook from the machine of performance. We created a permission slip for rest: unstructured mornings, slow walks without a goal, afternoons spent sketching for no one but herself. At first, it felt unbearable, she described the silence as "too loud." But over time, her nervous system began to settle.

Through solitude, she reconnected with her body's natural rhythm. Through rituals of rest, she began to feel color and sensation return to her work, not as an obligation, but as a sacred extension of her being. Her creative block dissolved not because she pushed through it, but because she *sat with* it.

"I thought I was broken," Isabel reflected. "But really, I was just exhausted from trying to earn my right to be."

Now, Isabel speaks openly about the power of solitude in her artistic and personal life. She doesn't just create beautiful work; she lives a life that honors the wholeness of who she is.

**Reflection Questions**

1. What have you been taught about the value of solitude?

2. When you're alone, do you feel peace or pressure? Why do you think that is?

3. How has productivity shaped your sense of self-worth or identity?

4. What does "care beyond productivity" mean to you personally?

5. What is one small way you could honor your soul today with no outcome attached?

CHAPTER 8

# HOW TO CHASE BIG DREAMS WITHOUT MELTING DOWN

You carry big dreams. Maybe they've lived quietly inside you for years, or maybe they surge forward in bursts of inspiration that take your breath away. Your vision is expansive, vivid, and often ahead of its time. That's the nature of your gifted, neurodivergent mind, it sees what could be, even when the world around you can't yet imagine it.

With your brilliance can come a deep and painful overwhelm. The pressure of the dream itself and the weight of details along with uncertainty of how to begin. One moment you are soaring with possibility, the next you are frozen, tangled in perfectionism, decision fatigue, or sensory and emotional overload. This doesn't mean you're broken. It means your nervous system is alert to every layer, every nuance. You are not just thinking of a dream, you are feeling it in full color. This intensity, when unsupported, can lead you to burnout before your first step is even taken.

So how do you honor your big dreams without burning out? You start by creating safety for yourself inside the dream. Break the vision down into gentle, sustainable pieces. Anchor it to your values. Let it breathe. Let it unfold at a pace that respects your energy cycles and your need for integration.

You don't need to do everything at once. You don't even need to know the whole plan. Begin with one clear step that feels manageable, not impressive, not perfect, just real. Progress doesn't require a spectacle. It requires steadiness, alignment, and enough nervous system regulation to stay in your body while you build.

Protect your energy as fiercely as you protect your dream. That means saying no to urgency culture, resisting the myth that "faster is better," and honoring your need for rest, play, and support. Build breaks into your process. Celebrate small wins. Surround yourself with people who see the *real* you, not just your output.

Let the dream evolve. You're not here to prove anything. You're here to create something meaningful on your terms, in your time, with your full humanity intact. You get to want more without sacrificing your well-being. You get to build something big without abandoning yourself. Your nervous system, your intuition, and your joy are not obstacles to success, they are your compass.

Keep going, gently. Dream big, move slow, and remember: the dream is about how you feel while you are creating your dream beyond thoughts alone.

## The Dreamer's Dilemma

There is a deep ache in the soul of the neurodivergent dreamer, the one who sees a better future, who feels the possibilities vibrating in their bones, who cannot *not* reach for more. But chasing big dreams, especially in a world that demands conformity and hustle, often comes with a cost: burnout, overwhelm, isolation, and the quiet fear that you are too much for this world. Many gifted and neurodivergent adults carry immense vision but lack safe, sustainable pathways to live those visions fully.

As an Intuitive Gifted Mentor, I've worked with brilliant, visionary adults whose sensitivity and drive collide in painful ways. They tell me, *"I know what I'm here to do, but I don't know how to keep going without breaking myself."* What they're really saying is: *How can I serve my calling without sacrificing my well-being?*

The answer lies not in shrinking your dream but in learning how to carry it with care. You must build scaffolding that honors your energy cycles, supports emotional integration, and reflects your authentic wiring. Dreaming big isn't the problem. Not knowing how to regulate your brilliance is where meltdowns happen.

## When Vision Becomes a Burden

Big dreams require clarity, but they also require pacing. For the neurodivergent soul, especially those wired for urgency, novelty, and justice, there's a pull to *do it all now*. But without internal regulation and intentional boundaries, the dream becomes a source of exhaustion rather than expansion.

One of the most vital teachings I share with clients is this: You don't have to earn your dream by burning out. You can walk toward it with rhythm, support, and breath.

Here are some grounding truths for the visionary neurodivergent adult:

- Urgency is often a trauma echo, not a soul directive.
- Rest is not a reward, it's a requirement.
- You are allowed to slowly build.
- You don't need to chase your dream; you need to be aligned.

When your nervous system feels safe, your intuition can guide your action. When your self-worth is intact, you can say no without guilt. When your life is built on soul care, your dream grows with you, not against you.

## Meet Michael

Michael is a 54-year-old C-suite executive at a rapidly expanding tech firm. He was widely respected in his industry, brilliant, intuitive, and relentlessly driven. Outwardly, he had it all. Internally, he was unraveling.

Michael came to me when his body began sending unmistakable signals: insomnia, gut issues, and migraines. He'd been powering through for decades. Raised as a gifted child with ADHD in a high-achieving family, Michael learned early that success equaled survival.

"I have this vision for changing corporate leadership," he told me in our first session. "I want to create humane, intuitive workplaces, but I'm crumbling under the weight of it."

Together, we explored the gap between his values and his current pace. We identified where he was outsourcing his inner authority to external expectations. Through customized soul care rituals, nervous system support, and permission to *not be the savior*, Michael began to shift.

Instead of constantly overperforming, he delegated. Instead of reacting to crises, he paused and resourced. His leadership didn't weaken; it matured. His team noticed his clarity. His family noticed his presence. Most importantly, he stopped melting down and started leading from wholeness.

Big dreams can light the way forward, but only when pursued with integrity to your unique rhythm. As you learn to carry your vision with grounded intention, you begin to recognize what you actually need to thrive, and what you can release. In the next chapter, we'll explore what it means to befriend your energy, so you can work *with* yourself instead of against yourself on the path to purpose. Michael's story reminds us that the bigger the dream, the deeper the roots must go.

## Reflection Questions

1. Where in your life are you chasing your dream from a place of urgency or fear, rather than alignment and care?

2. What internal or external messages are you still believing that say you must "earn" your dream through overwork or sacrifice?

3. How does your body signal that you're nearing the edge of burnout? Are you listening?

4. In what ways might slowing down actually support the growth of your dream?

5. What kind of support system would allow you to carry your vision more sustainably?

# CHAPTER 9

# THE RHYTHM OF YOUR ENERGY IS UNIQUE TO YOU

You are not wired like everyone else, and you were never meant to be. The way your energy flows, rises, and falls has its own tempo. It does not follow the rigid lines of the calendar or the pressure of the clock. It follows your nervous system, your inner seasons, your lived experience.

You may have bursts of brilliance followed by stillness. You may move in spirals rather than straight lines. You may come alive at unusual hours, or need more quiet space to process, recover, or simply *be*. This is not a flaw. This is not something to fix. This is your rhythm. It is valid. It is wise.

You've probably been told to ignore it. Push through. Fit in. Conform to schedules and standards that were never designed for your neurodivergent mind. Maybe you've tried. Maybe you've succeeded at performing "normal" for a while. But deep down, you feel the cost. Exhaustion. Frustration. Disconnection from yourself. It's time to honor your natural energy instead of overriding it.

Notice when you feel most alive. Pay attention to what drains you. Track the cycles daily, weekly, monthly and without judgment. Let yourself move in harmony with your own current, not in competition with someone else's pace.

You are allowed to rest before you're depleted. You are allowed to slow down when the world speeds up. You are allowed to build a life that supports your energy rather than one that constantly demands more than you can give.

When you align with your natural rhythm, clarity emerges. Decisions feel lighter. Motivation returns. Your body exhales. You stop fighting yourself and begin partnering with your inner knowing.

There is no single "right" way to structure your day, your work, or your rest. What works for others may not work for you and that's not a problem. It's a truth to build around. The goal is not maximum efficiency. The goal is sustainable aliveness.

You have permission to shape your days around how you function best, not how you have been told you should function. Your energy is beautifully receptive and responsive. Your unique patterns are not wrong or unpredictable. It speaks a language your soul understands. All you need to do is listen. Trust what you hear. And allow that rhythm to guide how you move through the world.

**Learning How to Honor Your Tempo**

If you are neurodivergent, gifted, or highly sensitive, chances are your energy doesn't move in straight lines or match societal expectations. You may move in bursts, periods of hyperfocus or high output followed by deep depletion. Or you may require extended solitude, varied sensory input, or spontaneous shifts in order to feel balanced. The rhythm of your energy is not linear. It is seasonal. Cyclical. Alive. Vibrant.

Yet for most of your life, you've probably been told, explicitly or implicitly, that your rhythm is wrong. That you are lazy if you need rest. That you're unreliable if your energy shifts. That something is *broken* in you because you can't perform at a steady, predictable pace like others.

The rhythm of your energy is not a flaw. It is your truth. When you honor it, you begin to thrive. Your energy is not meant to serve capitalism or conformity. It is meant to serve your well-being, your creativity, and your calling. In my mentoring work, I guide clients to unlearn the belief that they must be "on" all the time and to discover what their unique rhythm actually is and then trust this inner knowing.

## The Harm of Energy Masking

Many neurodivergent adults live in chronic overwhelm. You may find yourself forcing energy you don't have smiling when you're overstimulated, responding when you're spent, pushing through when your entire being is asking you to slow down. You show up to tasks, meetings, or conversations out of habit, out of pressure, out of survival conditioning. You mimic the cadence and pace of those around you, trying to keep up with rhythms that don't reflect your own. It works until it doesn't.

This kind of masking creates an invisible fracture between your outer life and your inner truth. Over time, that fracture deepens into disconnection, chronic stress, emotional numbness, or physical illness. Your body begins to speak louder. Your soul begins to ache. Still, you may wonder, *"Why can't I just keep going like everyone else"?* The truth is: you're not supposed to.

You were never designed to function in a linear, uniform way. Your energy is cyclical, responsive, and often nonlinear. It fluctuates based on sensory input, emotional intensity, creative inspiration, and nervous system capacity. That variability is not a flaw. It's a form of intelligence. Think of your energy like the tide. It doesn't apologize for coming in slowly or pulling back to regroup. Each phase has purpose. Each ebb creates the space for a future swell.

You may experience:
- Intense focus that needs recovery on the other side
- Social bursts followed by deep solitude
- Creative sparks at midnight instead of 9 a.m.
- The need for stillness after overstimulation, even when others are pressing forward

You are not inconsistent, you are attuned.

The more you ignore your natural rhythm, the more your system will rebel. The more you honor it, the more capacity you'll reclaim. Building your life around your energy does not require a complete overhaul. It begins with small permission: saying no without guilt, scheduling downtime without needing to earn it, noticing when your energy dips instead of shaming yourself for it.

This is not about doing less. It is about doing differently. Doing in a way that doesn't cost you your wellness, your clarity, or your soul.

You get to create a life that meets *you* where you are not where others expect you to be. That is not avoidance. That is integrity. That is healing. This is how you stop leaking energy and start living whole.

## Meet Richard

Richard is a 39-year-old creative entrepreneur who came to me feeling like a failure. "I can never stay consistent," he said. "I'm either all in or completely out of steam. I worry I'll never be successful."

As we worked together, Richard began to track his energy patterns instead of judging them. He noticed that his most creative ideas came late at night, after long walks, and rarely during meetings. He realized he wasn't flaky; he was rhythmic. His "inconsistency" was actually a deep internal pattern trying to emerge and assert itself.

We began restructuring his work around this truth. He shortened his meetings, scheduled downtime after launches, and added movement and meditation into his days. As a result, he was able to sustain creative work without crashing. His inner critic softened. His health improved. And his business began to grow organically on his terms.

Richard learned what so many of us must learn and understand: Your rhythm is a guide, not a problem to fix.

When we embrace the rhythm of our energy rather than resist it, we begin to reclaim our time, our vitality, and our truth. This self-attunement is a radical act of care in a world that constantly pushes for more. In the next chapter, we'll explore the sacred importance of saying no, not as rejection, but as a reclamation of your energy, your values, and your soul's direction.

## Reflection Questions

1. What messages have you internalized about what your energy "should" look like?

2. When in your life have you felt most aligned with your natural rhythm? What helped support that alignment?

3. What parts of your daily routine feel like they fight against your energy, and what could shift?

4. How does your energy tend to move through the day, the week, or the seasons? Have you ever tracked or honored that?

5. What would it feel like to believe that your unique energy pattern is *valid*, even if no one else understands it?

CHAPTER 10

# THE SACRED POWER OF SAYING NO

For your neurodivergent soul, "no" is often a word loaded with fear, shame, or discomfort. Many of us were trained to say yes: to please, to perform, to prove our worth. We learned early that *approval was given in exchange for compliance.* But what if saying no is not a rejection of others, but a deep act of devotion to yourself?

Saying no, especially as a gifted or intensely sensitive person, is rarely about defiance. Saying No as a Form of Soul Protection. It's about discernment. It's about identifying the people, spaces, commitments, and energies that deplete your system and having the courage to protect your precious inner world. In my work, I often say: *"Your yes means nothing if your no isn't trusted."*

The truth is, every time you say yes when you mean no, you abandon yourself a little. You disconnect from your body, your energy, and your intuition. Over time, this self-betrayal can lead to chronic resentment, exhaustion, and confusion about who you really are.

Boundaries are not barriers. Both inner and outer boundaries are bridges to authenticity. And "no" is one of the clearest boundary-setting tools we have. This simple 2-letter word, well used, offers us an opening to competence and confidence in the use of our boundaries.

**The Deep Need for Boundaries**
For neurodivergent people, boundaries are not just helpful, they are essential. The world is often too fast, too loud, too demanding.

Without boundaries, your nervous system lives in a constant state of alert. You feel everything. You sense undercurrents others miss. And without containers to hold your energy, life becomes a slow erosion of your clarity, joy, and vitality.

But let's be honest: boundaries can feel threatening to those who benefit from your lack of them. That's why so many gifted and intensely sensitive adults avoid setting boundaries until a crisis forces them to evaluate their rules of engagement. The key is to start from a place of self-loyalty rather than self-defense.

Here's what healthy boundaries can sound like:
- "I'm not available for that but thank you for thinking of me."
- "I need time to consider before giving you an answer."
- "That doesn't work for me right now."
- "I'm at capacity. I won't be able to take that on."
- "I'm stepping away so I can reconnect with myself."

Boundaries don't have to be harsh to be effective. In fact, the most powerful boundaries are calm, clear, and consistent. They come from a place of *knowing who you are* and *what you need to stay healthy and whole*.

Squishy boundaries can cause disruptions in your sense of peace and wellbeing. Squishy boundaries send mixed messages to others and yourself which then causes discord and a lack of authentic rapport. Boundaries are fluid and having firm, compassionate parameters make for healthy engagement and self-respect.

## Why It Is Hard (Especially for the Gifted & Sensitive)

Neurodivergent individuals often carry heightened empathy. You feel others' needs. You see what must be done. You anticipate the impact of your boundary before you even speak. This can make it excruciating to choose yourself.

Add in perfectionism, trauma, or the conditioning of being the "smart one" or "helper," and saying no can feel like failure. Yet saying yes to everything dilutes your purpose and drains your nervous system of its vital life force.

Your physical energy is not infinite. Your time is not disposable. Your gifts are not owed to everyone. When you say no with clarity and compassion, you're not closing a door, you're opening space for what's aligned, generative, and reciprocal.

## Healthy Ways to Say No
You don't have to justify, over-explain, or apologize for your "no". You can simply state it with grounded clarity. Here are some healthy ways to express a "no" that respects both yourself and the other person:
- "That's not something I can take on right now."
- "I'm honored you asked, and I'm going to pass this time."
- "I need to protect my energy and say no to this request."
- "This isn't aligned with my current priorities."
- "I'd rather not commit to that but thank you."

It's okay to say "no" even if you're available. It's okay to say "no" even if they don't understand. What matters most is your inner alignment and long-term well-being.

Saying no is not about being rigid, it is about being grounded in your sense of who you are. As you honor your boundaries, you begin to live from the inside out, rather than from the outside in. This creates space for joy, clarity, and alignment.

## Meet Jared
Jared is a 51-year-old nonprofit director whose passion for service had quietly turned into self-erasure. When he first came to me, he looked exhausted not just physically, but deep in his soul. "I love the mission," he told me, "But I can't keep sacrificing myself for it. I feel guilty setting limits, but I also feel like I'm disappearing."

Beneath the surface, the pattern was clear. Jared's "*no*" had been silenced for years, buried beneath a lifetime of performance, perfectionism, and people-pleasing. He had internalized the belief that being needed was the same as being worthy. He feared that if he did not over-deliver, he would let people down or worse, be seen as replaceable.

Our work together wasn't about teaching him how to be productive again. It was about helping him remember his own center.

We began with small, consistent acts of boundary repair. Jared practiced saying *no* to meetings that drained him and yes to rest that restored him. He shortened his workdays, even when it felt uncomfortable. He learned to pause mid-conversation when sensory or emotional overwhelm crept in. These weren't dramatic gestures. They were gentle reclaiming of his time, space, and nervous system.

Slowly, his body responded. His sleep deepened. His mind quieted. He started writing again something he hadn't done in over a decade. His staff noticed the shift and began honoring his time more readily. He didn't have to justify or explain his energy spoke for itself.

Jared didn't become less committed to his mission. He became more rooted in his own truth. More present. More honest. His generosity didn't shrink; it sharpened. He began leading from fullness rather than depletion.

For Jared, "no" was no longer a rejection. It became a sacred act of care boundary that protected what mattered most, including himself. And for the first time in years, he stopped vanishing in service to the cause and started showing up as his whole self, unapologetically.

**Reflection Questions**

1. In what areas of your life do you struggle to say no, even when you want to?

2. What stories have you been told (or told yourself) about what saying no means about you?

3. What do you fear will happen if you say no? How often do those fears actually come true?

4. What is one area of your life where a boundary could bring more peace or freedom?

5. How would your life change if you trusted your no as much as your yes?

# CHAPTER 11

# THE ART OF SUSTAINABLE CONTRIBUTION

You are someone who gives deeply. Your contributions often go beyond what others can see, energetic labor, emotional presence, creative insight, careful listening. You sense what's needed and you offer it, often before anyone asks. While this capacity to give is beautiful, it can also become depleted if not balanced by something essential: reciprocity.

Reciprocity an energetic agreement that what you give is met with care, respect, or acknowledgment in return. It is the flow that keeps your nervous system from entering survival mode. It's the pattern that says: you matter too. Reciprocity is not about keeping score. It's not a mere transaction. There is an energy flow that holds reverence for all concerned, including our Earth and nature herself.

When reciprocity is absent, your giving starts to erode you. You may find yourself giving more to hold things together, absorbing others' discomfort, picking up slack, or minimizing your own needs to preserve harmony. Over time, this leads to resentment, burnout, and even illness. Your contribution becomes unsustainable, not because you're weak, but because you are living in a unidimensional landscape and are blinded to the value of or living with reciprocity being your guide.

Sustainable contribution honors your limits. It allows you to check in and ask: *Is there flow here? Is my giving being met? Do all involved feel nourished in this exchange?* Sometimes reciprocity looks like being paid fairly. Sometimes it's a heartfelt thank you. Sometimes it's being heard, supported, or simply seen in return. Whatever form it takes, you're allowed to ask for it. You're allowed to expect it. Not because you're demanding, but because you're human, and because the gifts you offer deserve to land in spaces where they're valued.

Reciprocity is not selfish. It is sacred balance. It affirms that your presence is not a resource to be drained, but a relationship to be honored. Your contribution will always be more powerful and more sustainable when it flows from mutual care. Let yourself receive. Let yourself be poured into, too.

## Offering Without Over Giving

Gifted and neurodivergent adults are often wired for their contribution. You see what needs to be fixed, elevated, healed, or transformed. You care deeply. You bring ideas, empathy, and intensity to every table you sit at. But without clear inner guidance and sustainable practices, your desire to contribute can become a trap, one that leads to over giving, depletion, and even resentment.

Sustainable contribution is not about giving less; it's about giving differently. It is the art of discerning what yours is to offer, how much of it you can give, and when to step back and replenish. It means offering from your overflow, not your core reserves.

In the dominant culture, contribution is often linked to performance and productivity. But soul-aligned contribution asks something else: Are you in right relationship with your energy, your purpose, and your community?

Many of the gifted and sensitive clients I've worked with grew up equating their worth with usefulness. They became the "fixers," the "listeners," the "helpers." The pattern becomes automatic: "If I'm not giving something valuable, I might disappear."

The truth is that your presence is inherently valuable. You don't have to pour yourself out to prove this to anyone, including yourself.

## Redefining Impact

One of the myths we must unlearn is that impact requires exhaustion. Some of the most transformative contributions you can make are subtle. They may be a well-placed insight, a steady presence, a clear boundary, a creative offering that arrives right on time.

Your nervous system, your joy, your health, these are all indicators of sustainable impact.

Here are some signs that your contribution is aligned:
- You feel energized rather than drained after giving
- You're not rescuing or over-functioning for others
- You give with clarity, instead of obligation
- Your giving includes *yourself* in the equation

Here are signs that your contribution has become unsustainable:
- You feel irritable, resentful, or unseen
- You keep saying yes while feeling internally depleted
- You lose track of your own needs
- You use giving as a way to avoid your own emotions or healing

Remember: You can contribute meaningfully without sacrificing your inner world... Always give from your overflow.

## Meet Eva

Eva is a 46-year-old educator and community advocate who came to me in a state of quiet collapse. She had poured years into serving marginalized youth, working evenings and weekends, often without pay. "If I stop," she said, "who will do it?"

We explored her deeper motives, part of her felt she had to make up for all the times she had been dismissed as a gifted, undiagnosed ADHD child. She didn't want anyone else to feel that pain. But her contribution had become martyrdom.

Together, we built a new rhythm. She began to mentor younger teachers instead of doing everything herself. She limited evening events. She carved out weekends for nature, rest, and art. And slowly, she realized: "My work deepens when I am nourished".

Eva began leading from her wholeness, not her wounds. And the result? Her impact grew not because she worked harder, but because she became more present, more grounded, and more discerning.

**Practices for Sustainable Contribution**

Here are a few practices to help you offer your gifts without losing yourself:

- **The Sacred Yes Filter**: Before saying yes, pause. Ask: Do I have the energy? Is this aligned with my values? Is it mine to do?
- **Contribution Calendar**: Track what, where, and how often you give. Does it feel joyful or obligatory? Adjust as needed
- **Daily Receiving Rituals**: Whether it's silence, nature, breathwork, or simply pleasure—commit to receiving as much as you give.
- **Know Your Limits**: Schedule rest before you need it. Learn your early signs of burnout and respond with care.
- **Let Others Contribute Too**: The world doesn't rest on your shoulders. Invite others into co-creation.

When your contribution arises from alignment rather than urgency, it becomes a powerful force of healing and influence. You begin to create from your essence, not from burnout or overwhelm. In the next chapter, we'll explore The Necessity of Joy and Play as vital sources of regulation, connection, and renewal for the neurodivergent soul. This goes far beyond the idea of joy and play being a simple luxury.

**Reflection Questions**

1. In what areas of your life are you or have you over-contributed or giving more than feels sustainable? In what ways have you taken more than your fair share of resources?

2. What beliefs do you hold about your worth and usefulness?

3. When have you contributed from a place of overflow rather than depletion and what changed?

4. What are three ways you can nourish yourself this week as a sacred act of balance?

5. Who, currently in your life, can and will support you in staying aligned with your sustainable pace and purpose?

# CHAPTER 12

# THE NECESSITY OF JOY AND PLAY

You were never meant to outgrow joy. Somewhere along the way, you may have been told that maturity means seriousness, that real learning requires discipline, that play is a distraction from purpose. But the truth is, joy and play are among the most powerful tools you have for growth, for vitality, and for staying connected to your inner spark.

Play activates curiosity. It invites experimentation without fear of failure. It opens the nervous system, making new ideas easier to receive and integrate. When you allow yourself to play freely, without an agenda, you create the conditions for learning that are embodied, intuitive, and lasting.

Joy fuels youthfulness. Not the kind measured in years, but the kind that radiates from within when your spirit is alive. When you laugh, explore, make something just because you want to, you reconnect to the part of you that is timeless. You become more open, more engaged, more willing to stretch into the unfamiliar. This is restoration. This isn't regression.

Let yourself chase what delights you. Let yourself move, color, sing, wonder, tinker. Whether you're building something, learning a new skill, or simply giving your brain a break, joy is not the reward, it is part of the process. The more joy you invite in, the more space you create for sustainable expansion.

You are allowed to learn like a child again. You are allowed to grow without grinding. Joy doesn't make you less serious, it makes your learning more alive.

## Joy Is Not Optional, It's Oxygen

In a world that rewards seriousness, productivity, and perfection, joy is often dismissed as childish or self-indulgent. But for the neurodivergent soul, especially those who are gifted, sensitive, or intense, joy and play are not luxuries. They are lifelines.

Play is how we regulate. Joy is how we remember who we are. These states aren't distractions from the "real work", they *are* the real work. Without joy, the soul withers. Without play, creativity and healing stall. For many gifted and neurodivergent adults, the path to reconnection with self begins not with doing more, but with reclaiming wonder.

Play doesn't just mean games or hobbies. It means engaging the world with curiosity, with lightness, with openness. It is a way of unmasking. A return to essence. A relief from the weight of always being "on."

In my work, I often remind clients: Play is how the nervous system exhales. Joy is a form of expressing your inner truth.

## The Impact of Joy Deprivation

Many neurodivergent people learned early that joy must be earned. You were taught to be useful, productive, and serious in order to be seen as valid. Maybe your joy was misunderstood or even punished. Maybe your creativity was called "too much." Over time, this breeds joy deprivation, a chronic undernourishment of the soul.

Without joy:
- We forget why we started
- Our creativity dulls
- Relationships feel transactional
- Life becomes an endurance test instead of a lived experience

When we begin to reintroduce joy and play in our lives, not just on weekends or holidays but woven through our days, something magical happens: the soul begins to bloom again. Reserving joy for some future time or activity is a form of self-denial. Joy is your natural state and is designed to be expressed through you as you.

## Meet Sophie

Sophie is a 42-year-old neurodivergent consultant who came to me after a health crisis left her unable to work. "I don't know how to rest," she admitted. "Even when I'm not working, my mind is in overdrive. I've forgotten how to feel joy."

Sophie had spent her life being the responsible one. She excelled in school, held leadership positions, and ran a successful business. But the cost had been immense: chronic tension, migraines, emotional numbness. Her body forced a reckoning.

We didn't start with goal setting. We started with joy. I asked her: "When did you last laugh without self-consciousness?" It had been years. We reintroduced small moments of play, coloring outside the lines, dancing barefoot in her kitchen, watching animated films that used to make her laugh as a child. At first, it felt awkward. But slowly, joy became a companion again.

Sophie's health stabilized. Her spark returned. Perhaps most importantly, she remembered who she was underneath all the striving: a playful, wildly imaginative, soulful human being.

## Sophies's Everyday Practices of Joy and Play

You don't have to wait until you've "earned" rest to feel joy. Here are some simple, everyday ways to reintroduce joy and play into your life:

- **Micro-joys**: Notice small pleasures, a favorite scent, a breeze, a warm drink. Let them register in your nervous system.
- **Unstructured time**: Block off time with no agenda. Let your curiosity lead.
- **Movement for pleasure**: Dance, sway, stretch, not for fitness, but for delight.
- **Create without outcome**: Paint, build, sing, write, doodle with no goal except self-expression.

- **Laugh without guilt**: Watch something silly. Call someone who makes you laugh. Give your seriousness a break.

Joy rewires your brain. Play repairs your soul. Joy reconnects us with our vitality. Play restores our presence. When we engage the world with wonder, we remember that we are more than our responsibilities, we are radiant, complex beings here to *live*, not just survive.

**Reflection Questions**

1. What was joyful to you as a child that you no longer allow yourself to experience?

2. How do you typically respond when you feel playful or silly, do you welcome it or shut it down?

3. What beliefs do you hold about joy that may be limiting your access to it?

4. What are three small ways you could invite more joy into your week starting now?

5. How does your body respond when you are truly at play?

# CHAPTER 13

# THE QUIET POWER OF SOLITUDE

Solitude and isolation are very different indeed. In a culture that often equates busyness with worth and extroversion with health, solitude can be misunderstood and even pathologized. But for the gifted, the neurodivergent, the intensely sensitive, solitude is not just a preference. It is a sacred necessity.

Solitude allows the overstimulated nervous system to settle down and decompress. It makes space for clarity, integration, and inner connection. It's where your intuition speaks the loudest and your soul gets the chance to exhale.

You are not broken for needing more space than others. You are not antisocial because you are craving stillness. You are not failing if you feel overwhelmed by constant interaction. Many of us have internalized the idea that we must always be available, responsive, or outwardly engaged, yet solitude is a portal back to ourselves.

Time alone without the pressure to perform, produce, or explain can restore your energy, sharpen your insight, and deepen your sense of purpose.

**Why Neurodivergent Souls Need Solitude**
The neurodivergent experience often includes heightened sensory perception, emotional attunement, and cognitive depth. Being around others, even when enjoyable, can lead to overstimulation.

Without adequate time to process and reset, overwhelm builds and can steal your joy and enthusiasm for life.

## Solitude offers:
- A buffer from sensory input
- Space to integrate emotional experiences
- A return to your own pacing and rhythm
- Freedom from masking or managing others' reactions
- A deeper connection to your inner wisdom and imagination

Many adults who were praised for their performance and adaptability were never taught how to rest into solitude. Instead, silence may have felt like loneliness, failure, laziness, or rejection. Healing your relationship with solitude is a profound reclamation. Your life will be transformed in ways you may not be able to imagine.

## Stepping Away: Making Space for True Solitude
You live in a world that never stops asking for your attention. Notifications, pings, scrolling feeds, endless tabs open, not just on your screen, but in your mind. It's easy to confuse stimulation with connection, distraction with rest. But the truth is, constant input keeps you from hearing your own voice.

Solitude begins when you step away, not just physically, but energetically. Turning off the screen is not a rejection of the world. It is a return to yourself. It is a sacred pause where your nervous system can exhale, and your inner landscape can speak.

You don't have to disappear for days. Even a few intentional minutes away from devices can open space for clarity, for grounded presence, for that deep kind of listening that only happens in stillness. These moments are where insights land, where creativity awakens, where your system finds its rhythm again.

You are allowed to unplug without guilt. You are allowed to not respond right away. You are allowed to rest from the noise and choose your own pace. Solitude is not about isolation—it is about re-centering. It's where you remember that you are whole without performing, producing, or pleasing.

Let the quiet hold you. Let your thoughts stretch out without interruption. Let your body be still without a screen to fill the space. In this gentle retreat, you are not missing out. You are tuning in. What you find there is more than enough.

**How to Make Solitude Nourishing**
Solitude isn't just about being alone, it's about being with yourself in a conscious, compassionate, caring and deeply loving way. Here are some practices that can support your solitude:
- **Unplug with intention**: Turn off devices for a set period each day. Let silence return to your life.
- **Create a sanctuary**: A room, corner, or even a chair that signals solitude and peace.
- **Journaling as presence**: Meet yourself on the page and allow inner reflection. This type of journaling is not a to-do list or one for productivity.
- **Nature as companion**: Walk without a destination. Let the earth steady your breath.
- **Soul questions**: Ask yourself meaningful questions, listen to your still small voice within and allow your answers to gently surface and then arrive over time in ways you will be able to understand.

Solitude is where integration happens. It's where the noise clears and your truth rises.

**Meet Marvin**
Marvin is a 55-year-old highly sensitive CEO whose life had become a blur of constant interaction. When he first came to me, his nervous system was frayed, his energy threadbare. "There's no quiet in my life," he said. "Even my downtime is filled with meetings, texts, and notifications. I'm exhausted, but I don't know how to step away without feeling guilty.".

Marvin wasn't just dealing with overstimulation. He was grappling with an old, unspoken fear, *"What happens if I stop"?* As we worked together, the root of that fear began to surface solitude had long been associated with abandonment. In his childhood, being alone didn't mean restoration, it meant neglect, emotional disconnection, being forgotten. No wonder he filled every corner of his schedule with people, noise, and tasks. The silence had once felt unsafe.

With care and gentleness, we began to reframe that silence. Marvin started with small, intentional moments, turning off his phone during meals, taking slow solo walks without a destination, journaling without a checklist or goal. At first, the quiet felt awkward. Then, it started to feel like oxygen.

Over time, something in him began to soften. "It's like I found the switch that dims the noise," he told me. He noticed he became less reactive in high-stakes meetings, more intuitive with his staff, and more emotionally centered in his personal life. He stopped micromanaging and started listening. His mornings became a sacred space for deep thinking and reflective planning, while his afternoons flowed with more clarity and ease.

Marvin didn't need to retreat from the world. He needed a rhythm that honored his sensitivity. He needed solitude, not as isolation, but as nourishment. A place to return to himself.

Through honoring his nervous system instead of overriding it, Marvin rediscovered his inner leadership. Not the one powered by hustle, but the one rooted in presence. The one that speaks when the world gets quiet.

## Reflection Questions

1. What comes up for you emotionally when you think about spending intentional time alone?

2. How do you currently use solitude as restoration, or as escape?

3. In what ways do you overextend socially to avoid being with your inner world?

4. What would a nourishing, joyful practice of solitude look like for you?

5. What wisdom might be trying to reach you, if only you created the space to listen?

PART 3

# UNDERSTANDING THE NEURODIVERGENT SOUL

## CHAPTER 14

# INTRICATE MINDS: SHARED LANDSCAPE OF GIFTEDNESS, ADHD, AND AUTISM

You live in a mind that does not follow the standard map. You sense, feel, and perceive in layers that others may not see. You've likely spent a lifetime trying to make sense of this complexity, trying to find the right labels, the right language, the right rhythm in a world that often reduces what it cannot understand.

Giftedness, ADHD, and autism are often treated as separate paths, with their own definitions and diagnostic boundaries. But lived experience tells a different story. These identities often coexist, overlap, or blur entirely. You may see yourself in more than one. You may feel like you belong to all, yet fully to none. And that ambiguity can feel both liberating and lonely.

You are not imagining this. The mind you inhabit is intricately wired for intensity, depth, and nuance. And there is nothing wrong with that.

You may have heard that giftedness is a gift, that ADHD is a deficit, and that autism is a disorder. You may have internalized some of those messages without even realizing it. But here is the truth I want you to hold onto: none of these parts of you are broken. They are all expressions of your unique neurobiology in different languages of the same intricate mind.

Your giftedness is not just intellect. It is intuition, creativity, moral clarity, and emotional intensity. It allows you to see possibilities others miss. It brings vision, insight, and often a sense of responsibility that weighs heavier than most people understand.

Your ADHD may show up as racing thoughts, unfinished projects, or restless energy. But beneath the chaos is a dynamic, idea-generating engine. You are a pattern-seeker, a spontaneous problem-solver, a divergent thinker. You don't just think outside the box you never believed the box should have been there in the first place.

Your autistic traits may include sensory sensitivity, social exhaustion, deep focus, or a love of structure. They may offer you a profound connection to detail, honesty, and the beauty of consistency. You feel life vividly in color, in vibration, in sensation. You move through the world with a nervous system tuned to different frequencies. That is not dysfunction, it is a difference. These traits do not cancel each other out. They inform one another. They create a layered reality that is hard to explain but deeply felt.

You may feel "too much" for one world and "not enough" for another. You may have been misunderstood by clinicians, educators, even loved ones. Maybe they tried to fit you into a single category or told you that one part of your mind invalidated the others. You are not too complex to be understood; you simply haven't been mirrored clearly yet. This is why self-understanding matters. Not to box yourself in, but to give yourself language, context, and compassion.

You are allowed to hold multiple truths. You can be highly intuitive and deeply analytical. You can be spontaneous and crave routine. You can need stimulation *and* still be overwhelmed by too much input. You can thrive in solitude *and* ache for connection.

There is no singular formula for the gifted neurodivergent soul. There is only the unfolding path of self-recognition of making peace with your own wiring and learning how to care for it with tenderness and precision.

This chapter is about affirming the truth you already know, that your mind is layered, luminous, and worthy of understanding. As you navigate your days, I invite you to ask not "What's wrong with me?" but rather, "What is my system trying to tell me?" Let your rhythms, preferences, sensitivities, and strengths become sacred data. Let your self-awareness become a sanctuary, not a source of shame.

You do not need to fit into someone else's framework to be whole. You are already whole. You are already worthy of care, community, and clarity, exactly as you are. In the shared landscape of giftedness, ADHD, and autism, you are not lost. You are layered. You are real. You are not alone.

## Meet Liam

Liam is a 27-year-old artist and software developer who first started mentoring with me after, yet another project collapsed under the weight of his own perfectionism and executive dysfunction. Diagnosed in childhood with both giftedness and ADHD, and later in adulthood with autism, Liam had grown up carrying two conflicting internal narratives: *"You are brilliant"* and *"You are a mess."*

Liam's mind was a marvel, a living kaleidoscope of connections, visions, and insights. He could conceptualize entire systems in minutes, intuit solutions others couldn't even name, and perceive emotional undercurrents in conversations that others barely registered. And yet, daily life often felt like quicksand. Liam was dealing with deep existential loneliness and quiet desperation and emotional pain.

He struggled to organize his tasks, remember deadlines, or stay attentive in meetings that flattened ideas into bullet points. He experienced frequent sensory overwhelm in ordinary settings like grocery stores or staff events. When he tried to explain his experiences, he was met with blank stares or unhelpful advice: "Just make a checklist," "You're overthinking it," or worse, "You're too sensitive." This kept Liam continuing to mask and guard his internal experience, thus causing more separation from others.

By the time Liam sought mentoring, he had internalized a profound sense of shame. His giftedness felt like a cruel joke, an ability to see limitless possibilities paired with an inability to execute them "properly" by neurotypical standards. Liam was stuck in a cycle that was drowning him.

With my guidance, Liam began to deconstruct the painful myths and inner dialogue he had lived under:

- Seeing the spiral: He learned that his mind's nonlinear processing wasn't a flaw to be "fixed"; it was a spiral way of thinking that could create rich, layered outcomes when properly honored and engaged with in everyday life.
- Building bridges: Rather than forcing himself into rigid systems, Liam co-created structures with me that matched *his* way of thinking visual timelines, voice memos, sensory breaks, and flexible goal setting. Liam learned to excel using his gifts rather than despite them.
- Healing self-concept: Most critically, Liam began to see that the very intensity he had been punished for, his emotional depth, his sensory awareness, his endless questioning was not pathology. It was soul.

Through patient mentoring and deep inner work, Liam shifted from seeing himself as broken to seeing himself as complex. His projects became not linear tasks to be "completed" but living ecosystems to be tended, one breath at a time.

He no longer measured success by conformity. He began to measure it by authenticity, by how fully he could live in alignment with his true nature.

As I often remind my clients that You are not too much. You are more than the world knows how to measure. Embracing the complexity of your mind is not just an act of survival, it's a declaration of strength. It's the first bold step toward reclaiming your power and crafting a life that celebrates your unique brilliance. As you continue this journey, know that every twist and turn of your neurodivergent soul holds the potential for growth, creativity, and profound fulfillment. Your adventure has only just begun.

## Reflection Questions

1. When have you experienced your mind as both a source of brilliance and a source of struggle? How do you usually respond to that paradox within yourself?

2. What aspects of your neurodivergence have you learned to hide or mask to fit into environments that were not designed for you? What has it cost you to do so?

3. In what moments have you felt most misunderstood despite seeing and sensing so much? What might shift if you treated that sensitivity as a strength rather than a flaw?

4. Can you recall a time when your nonlinear thinking or pattern recognition offered insight others couldn't see? How might you fully honor that capacity in your daily life?

5. What would it look like to trust that your way of processing the world is not broken, but beautifully complex a forest to explore, rather than a path to fix?

## CHAPTER 15

# LIVING IN A WORLD NOT BUILT FOR YOU

To be neurodivergent is often to move through a world designed by and for the neurotypical majority. From the structure of school days to the pace of office life, from unspoken social rules to sensory environments flooded with noise and light, much of modern life demands a kind of masking, suppression, or contortion of one's natural rhythms just to get by.

For many, this creates a chronic state of internal dissonance. The external world says, to be faster, quieter, be more flexible, be less intense. The neurodivergent soul feels everything fully: change, injustice, inefficiency, beauty. When the world pushes you to override your internal compass again and again, you begin to lose your connection to it. Without that compass, disorientation and burnout often follow.

This dissonance isn't just cognitive, it's existential. The neurodivergent person often feels out of step with time itself. Too fast for slow systems. Too slow for fast ones. Too complex for simplistic solutions. Too sensitive for a culture addicted to desensitization.

There is grief here. Grief for the friendships that couldn't hold your intensity. For the classrooms where you were misdiagnosed or overlooked. For the jobs where your creativity was stifled in favor of "fitting in." Grief, too, for the parts of yourself you had to tuck away in order to be palatable to others.

Yet, this grief contains wisdom. In not fitting, you begin to see what is broken. In being forced to adapt, you begin to question what is worthy of adaptation. In being told to conform, you learn to discern where your soul ends and the conditioning begins.

To live in a world not built for you is a wound that can also offer a powerful perspective. From here, you can imagine what a different world might look like. One that honors slowness, celebrates divergence, invites nuance, and respects deep feeling.

Healing begins not in making yourself fit in the world, but in building a life, a space, a rhythm, and eventually a community that fits you. This is how you rectify the trajectory of your life and your daily experience.

## Accommodations Access Points

When the world around you is designed for a different rhythm, a different pace, and a different set of sensory expectations, navigating daily life can feel like walking uphill in shoes that don't fit. You may have spent years adapting, contorting, and overriding your own needs just to function, just to appear "capable." And while that kind of adaptation is often praised, it comes at a cost: your nervous system, your energy, your sense of ease.

Accommodations exist to shift that burden. They are not about getting an advantage; they are about restoring balance. They are about creating a world where *you* can participate without losing pieces of yourself in the process.

You are allowed to need things that others do not. Noise-canceling headphones, flexible deadlines, written instructions, time buffers between meetings, dimmer lights, fewer social demands, permission to stim, to move, to take breaks. These are not indulgences. These are bridges between your inner world and the outer one.

Too often, gifted and neurodivergent adults carry the belief that asking for accommodations means weakness. Especially if you've been high functioning, praised for your output, or the one others relied on. But needing support doesn't cancel your strengths. It sustains them.

You don't have to earn comfort. You don't have to justify your wiring. Accommodations are not about proving you deserve a different path, they are about honoring the one you already walk.

Asking for what you need clearly, without an apology is not a disruption. It is a declaration that your well-being matters. You are not here to survive a system that drains you. You are here to build a life that reflects your truth.

The world may not be built for you and that doesn't mean you cannot shape your corner of the world with clarity, care, and courage. Accommodations are one way you begin to create your safe environment for your success and fulfillment.

## Meet Maya

Maya is a 38-year-old gifted educator who shared that she has been diagnosed with autism and has spent most of her life feeling like an outsider in the very systems meant to support her growth. School was a gauntlet of sensory overload, rigid schedules, and unspoken social codes she struggled to decode. Her talents were often overlooked, and her struggles misinterpreted as willful disobedience or laziness.

As an adult, Maya found herself trapped in a corporate job that demanded constant multitasking, rapid meetings, and noisy open offices. The environment left her exhausted, disconnected from her own rhythms and deeply anxious. She masked her discomfort so effectively that colleagues often described her as "quiet but efficient," never realizing the internal chaos beneath the surface.

After years of pushing herself to conform, Maya began to experience chronic burnout and a gnawing sense of grief for the parts of herself she'd had to silence. She realized she no longer recognized the woman in the mirror, a soul diminished by relentless adaptation.

When Maya began mentoring with me, her first breakthroughs came from simply naming this dissonance. Together, we explored:

- The cost of masking: Maya acknowledged the emotional toll of living behind a carefully crafted façade.
- The loss and reclamation of rhythm: She reconnected with

her natural cycles of focus and rest, rather than forcing herself into the standard 9-to-5 grind.
- Distinguishing conditioning from essence: Maya began to discern which parts of her behaviors and beliefs were authentically hers, and which were adaptations born from survival.

With my support, Maya made courageous shifts: she transitioned to part-time work that honored her sensory needs, created a personal sanctuary at home for quiet reflection, and joined a community of neurodivergent peers who understood her experience.

Through these steps, Maya reclaimed her internal compass. No longer defined by what the world demanded, she began to live from a place of deep alignment with her true self, a profound healing that restored her soul's voice and vitality.

Living in a world not built for you can feel isolated and exhausting, but it also offers a unique perspective filled with insight and strength. By honoring your own rhythms and reclaiming your internal compass, you begin to build a life that truly fits, one rooted in authenticity, connection, and soulful care. As we continue, we will explore practical ways to nurture that life, creating spaces where your neurodivergent soul can not only survive but thrive.

**Reflection Questions**

1. Where in your life have you felt pressured to hide or reshape your natural rhythms in order to be accepted? How did that experience affect your sense of self?

2. What are some specific environments (school, work, social settings) where you felt "too much" or "not enough" In hindsight, what were those spaces missing that you needed?

3. What parts of yourself have you tucked away to be palatable to others, and what might it look like to begin reclaiming them? Are there small, safe ways you could start expressing them again?

4. What grief do you carry from the disconnect between who you are and what the world expected of you? Can you name that grief, honor it, and allow it to speak?

5. If you could build a life or space that truly fits *you*, what qualities would it have? What would it celebrate or honor that the mainstream often overlooks?

## CHAPTER 16

# SENSORY SENSITIVITY AND THE SOUL

Sensory sensitivity is often described clinically as a dysfunction, a processing disorder, or a problem to be managed. But what if we reframed it entirely? What if, instead of pathologizing it, you recognized this trait as a sacred language of your soul?

For the neurodivergent, the world is not simply observed, it is *felt* in full color, in immediate intensity. Light doesn't just illuminate; it *pierces*. Sound doesn't merely fill the air; it *vibrates* through the body. Textures speak, sometimes whispering comfort and sometimes shouting discomfort. Smells can evoke entire landscapes of memory, both joyful and jarring. In this immersive experience of reality, the nervous system is porous, and your soul absorbs everything.

This heightened attunement can be a nuanced gift. On one hand, it opens a gateway to wonder: the shimmer of wind through leaves, the precise tone of a loved one's voice, the way music can rise like prayer and settle like balm. It allows for intimacy with the present moment that often escapes a culture driven by numbness and distraction. On the other hand, this same gift, when misunderstood or invalidated, can lead to sensory overload, shutdown, and isolation.

Many neurodivergent people learn early on how to suppress their sensory needs in order to fit into the environment at large. You may have forced yourself into scratchy clothes, endure harsh lighting, push through bustling, overwhelming environments, all while absorbing the message that your experiences are "too much," "unreal," or "inconvenient." Over time, you learn to dissociate. The soul, muffled. Your cries go unheard. What should never have been endured becomes routine.

There is another path. A path that sees sensory sensitivity as wisdom rather than weakness. As a compass pointing toward your deeper truth. As a portal into a richer, more embodied reality.

When the soul is gently invited to reunite with the body through sensory reclamation, healing begins. Softness becomes a language. Weighted blankets, warm water, lavender-scented oils, rhythmic rocking, all these are essentials rather than luxuries. They are medicine. Grounding rituals become anchors. Sensory sanctuaries become altars. Embodied expression becomes the invitation home. This is the art of sensory stewardship: learning to care for a system that is exquisitely alive. You!

To be intensely sensitive is not fragile, it is where your authentic power lies. It is to be open and receptive while being profoundly connected to the invisible textures of existence.

## Meet Olivia

Olivia is a 38-year-old visual designer who came to mentoring sessions with me overwhelmed, fatigued, and deeply disconnected from her body. As a gifted and highly sensitive adult, she had spent years building a successful career, but at the cost of her wellbeing. She had been gaslighting her own body for decades, dismissing her needs for quiet, softness, and solitude in favor of pushing through noisy offices, overbooked schedules, and harsh lighting.

In our work together, Olivia hesitantly revealed a long history of being told she was "too dramatic" or "too sensitive." Her school years were filled with discomfort, fluorescent lighting made her nauseous, and she dreaded loud lunchrooms. As an adult, she mimicked what she saw others doing, all while secretly suffering from chronic migraines, digestive issues, and emotional numbness.

During our sessions, I guided Olivia in a practice of sensory awareness and self-permission. We co-created her first sensory sanctuary, a space in her home with low lighting, soft textures, grounding scents, and calming music. For the first time in years, she let her nervous system fully exhale.

As she explored this new relationship with her body, we worked on language: no longer referring to her needs as "quirks" or "issues," but instead as guidance. She began bringing small rituals into her workday: wearing noise-canceling headphones, using weighted lap pads, and incorporating movement breaks. Slowly, her body started to trust her again.

By the sixth month of mentoring, Olivia was not only functioning with more vitality she had reconnected with her creativity. Her artwork became more expressive, more intuitive. She told me, "For the first time, I don't feel like I'm fighting the world just to exist. I'm creating a world that fits me."

Olivia's story is not rare. It is the story of many sensitive souls who are waiting for permission to live fully in their skin and then discover that they have had permission all along.

As you begin to honor the sacred language of your sensory world, you uncover more than physical preferences, you touch the very edge of your emotional and empathic terrain. For the neurodivergent soul, sensory experiences are often interwoven with emotional resonance: a sound may trigger a memory, a texture may evoke a deep longing, a scent may stir unexpected grief. Just as the body feels deeply, so too does the heart. In the next chapter, we explore how emotional depth and empathy, while profound gifts, can also become sources of intense overwhelm and how learning to navigate this inner ocean with grace is essential for wholeness and soul care.

## Reflection Questions

1. When did you first receive the message that your sensory experiences were "too much" or inconvenient? How did that message shape the way you relate to your body and environment today?

2. Which sensory inputs sounds, textures, scents, lights feel nourishing and grounding to your system? How often do you allow yourself to intentionally seek them out?

3. Are there everyday situations where you push past your sensory limits in order to "get through" or blend in? What might it look like to pause and honor your body's signals in those moments instead?

4. What sensory-based practices or rituals bring you into greater alignment with your soul and nervous system? How can you begin to treat these not as luxuries, but as essential forms of soul care?

5. If your sensitivity were a sacred gift or a language of your soul, what might it be trying to communicate to you right now? What would it mean to listen more closely?

# CHAPTER 17

# EMOTIONAL DEPTH, EMPATHY, AND OVERWHELM

To be neurodivergent often means to feel not just your own emotions deeply but to sense and sometimes absorb the emotional undercurrents of those around you. This is not merely a psychological trait, but an energetic truth for many sensitive and gifted individuals. Emotional depth and empathy are hallmarks of the neurodivergent soul: intricate, intense, and often invisible to others.

Where some may feel a ripple, you may feel a tidal wave. Joy isn't just happiness, it's radiance. Grief doesn't merely sting; it echoes through your marrow. Injustice isn't just frustrating, it becomes unbearable. This depth brings great capacity for compassion, insight, and creativity, but it also comes with its own form of vulnerability.

Empathy, when untrained or unprotected, can lead to emotional enmeshment and burnout. You may find yourself overwhelmed not just by your own feelings, but by the silent sorrows, anxieties, or projections of others. Crowded rooms, relational tension, and global suffering can register not just as *concern*, but as crisis. Many gifted and sensitive people unconsciously internalize emotional energies that were never theirs to carry.

The world rarely teaches us how to manage this. More often, it tells us to "toughen up," "stop taking things so personally," or "let it go." But the truth is, emotional intensity is not a flaw to be fixed, it is a force to be channeled.

The healing begins when we understand that emotional depth is not the same as emotional dysregulation. Emotional intelligence does not require emotional suppression. The goal is not to feel less, but to feel wisely, to become fluent in the language of emotion without drowning in its current.

Empathy, too, must be reclaimed, not as boundaryless absorption, but as a sacred skill of attunement. You can learn when to open and when to close, when to witness and when to release. You can develop rituals for emotional cleansing, grounding, and energetic protection. You can choose to center your own nervous systems without abandoning your compassion. To feel deeply is to live fully when that depth is rooted in self-trust and discernment.

## When You Feel Everything: The Weight of Empathic Overwhelm

You feel deeply, not just your own emotions, but the emotions of everyone around you. You walk into a room and sense the undercurrents before a word is spoken. Your body absorbs tone, expression, tension, and silence. You may not always be able to explain it, but you know that knowing lives in your chest, your gut, your skin. This is the life of an empath. This is the sensitivity of an intuitive soul.

Your emotional depth is not imaginary, and it is not excessive. It is a form of wisdom, a way of reading the world beyond logic. Without grounding and support, being an empath can become exhausting. You may find yourself carrying what is not yours like other people's fears, grief, confusion, expectations. The line between where you end and others begin often gets blurred when you have squishy boundaries.

When you're gifted and neurodivergent and empathic, the world can feel like it is turned all the volume knobs up at once. You may feel pulled in many emotional directions, overwhelmed by subtleties that others don't even register. Because you often can hold space for others, they come to you over and over without realizing they are leaving you flooded with emotion or soul level tired. This is about your individual capacity. It has nothing to do with being weak or fragile and you may think. Just because you can feel it all doesn't mean you should. Just because you're capable of empathy doesn't mean you're here to be a vessel for everyone else's pain.

Overwhelm, for you, is not always about doing too much, it's often about feeling too much with no release. Your nervous system was not designed to be a constant receiver and absorber. You are allowed to protect your sensitivity. You are allowed to say, *not right now*. You are allowed to pause before responding. You are allowed to leave the room, turn off the phone, walk away from the energy that is not aligned with your peace.

Your intuition is a gift, but it is not meant to cost you your clarity. Your empathy is powerful, but it is not meant to deplete you. Emotional depth is sacred only when it's tended to with clear boundaries, self-trust, and gentleness.

Let yourself step back when needed. Let yourself rest from absorbing. Let yourself feel what's yours and release what isn't. This is how you stay whole. This is how you stay well. And this is how your emotional depth becomes not just a burden to bear, but a source of true connection, healing, and strength.

## Emotional Dysregulation and the Depth You Carry

You feel emotions in full color. When joy comes, it fills the room. When grief arrives, it settles in your bones. Your emotions are not at the surface level, they are immersive, layered, and alive. This depth is not dysfunction. It is part of how you process the world. Yet, the same emotional intensity that brings insight and beauty can also bring overwhelm. When your nervous system is already sensitive—due to giftedness, ADHD, autism, trauma, or a combination—regulating those big emotions can feel impossible. One small disruption can ripple into a storm. One word, one look, one piece of news can trigger a cascade that is hard to stop.

This is emotional dysregulation because your system processes everything. You don't just have emotions. You embody them. When the volume turns up too quickly, or there's no safe outlet, your body reacts with shutdown, meltdown, or spiraling anxiety. You may have been told you're overreacting. That you're too sensitive. That you need to toughen up or calm down. But those responses only deepen the shame and disconnection. What you actually need is support, spaciousness, and understanding. Your emotional reactions are signals, giving you vital information for regulation.

Regulation is about building practices that help you return to your center without abandoning your emotional truth. Breathwork, movement, co-regulation with safe people, and sensory grounding are tools and valuable lifelines. They are what allow you to stay present with your depth without drowning in emotion.

You don't need to become less feeling to be functional. You need systems of care that honor the reality of your nervous system and the beauty of your emotional landscape. Your emotional depth is a gift. When tended to with compassion and wisdom, it becomes one of your greatest sources of clarity, connection, and creativity. You are deeply alive and learning how to hold this reality with grace.

**Meet Marcus**
Marcus is a 42-year-old educator and coach who came to mentoring emotionally raw. On the surface, he was thriving, respected in his field, highly relational, and known for his wisdom. Yet privately, Marcus was exhausted. He told me, "I walk into a room, and I know instantly who's hurting, even if they don't say a word. By the end of the day, I feel like I've lived ten different lives and none of them are mine."

He shared stories of absorbing others' emotions so strongly that he would come home and cry without knowing why. As a child, Marcus was often praised for being mature and caring, but never taught how to release what he took in. Over time, his empathic gift became a silent burden. He'd stopped trusting his own emotional compass, unsure which feelings were truly his.

In our mentoring sessions, Marcus began to learn energetic hygiene: daily rituals to ground his own energy before and after work. We developed simple check-in practices: "Is this mine to feel?" became a mantra. He started using visualization to return emotional energy to its source, and we crafted a personal "empathic boundary" practice that involved breathwork, intention, and embodied awareness.

One of the most transformative moments came during a session where Marcus realized he had confused emotional openness with emotional availability. "I thought being empathic meant I had to say yes to everything to carry everyone. Now I see I can be deeply caring without sacrificing myself."

Marcus created a rhythm of solitude and silence as part of his self-care, giving his own emotions space to rise without interference. He rediscovered joy not because his feelings became lighter, but because they were *his own*. With time, Marcus began teaching these practices to his students, helping them hold their own emotional depth with dignity.

## Reflection Questions

1. When have you felt consumed by emotions that may not have been entirely your own? How did you recognize it?

2. What beliefs do you hold about empathy and emotional availability? Where might those beliefs need updating or reshaping?

3. What simple rituals could help you cleanse, release, or recalibrate your emotional energy on a regular basis?

4. How would your life change if you trusted your emotional depth instead of fearing it? What might become possible?

5. Who in your life honors your emotional depth and empathic nature, and who diminishes it? How might you set boundaries or seek connection that supports your authentic emotional experience?

CHAPTER 18

# THE MYTH OF BROKENNESS: UNLEARNING INTERNALIZED ABLEISM

Somewhere along the way, many neurodivergent souls begin to believe a lie: they tell themselves and others that they are broken. Not simply different, but defective. Not simply sensitive, but unstable. Not simply gifted, but impossible. This belief doesn't arise in a vacuum, it is cultivated by a society that measures human value through narrow, neurotypical standards of productivity, conformity, and emotional regulation.

Ableism, the belief that there is a "correct" way for minds and bodies to function is baked into the systems we live in: schools that prize sitting still, workplaces that reward uniformity, healthcare models that pathologize differences. When you're told repeatedly, implicitly or explicitly, that you are too much, too little, too scattered, too intense, it begins to seed a deep shame. Over time, the neurodivergent person internalizes these messages. They stop asking, "What's wrong with the system?" and start asking, "What's wrong with me?"

This is the myth of brokenness. And it is a lie that costs us our joy, our self-trust, and often our ability to imagine a life aligned with our truth.

In my work mentoring gifted, sensitive, and neurodivergent adults, I often witness the unspoken grief that comes from decades of internalized ableism. Clients describe a haunting sense of not belonging anywhere, even within themselves. They use language like "I'm a misfit," "I never got it right," or "I've always felt behind." This narrative is not born from truth; it's born from trying to force one's spirit into containers that were never designed to hold it. The healing begins not with fixing, but with unlearning.

Unlearning the cultural scripts that define value through output. Unlearning the emotional conditioning that says regulation means numbness. Unlearning the myth that to be different is to be disordered. This is not denial of challenges, this is the beginning of right relationship with our neurodivergent design.

What if we stopped viewing our sensitivity, intensity, and nonlinear ways of thinking as impairments, and instead began to see them as gifts that simply require different conditions to thrive? What if your meltdowns were not failures, but signs that you've been pushing past your limits in an unsafe environment? What if your procrastination was not laziness, but a clue about misalignment, fear, or sensory overwhelm?

Unlearning ableism means reclaiming your wholeness. It means listening to your own rhythms, redefining success on your terms, and resisting systems that ask you to abandon yourself in order to be accepted. You are not broken. You are breaking free of your old patterns and beliefs, allowing room for your new ways of being in the world.

**Meet Priya**

Priya is a 36-year-old nonprofit director who came into mentoring with what she described as "a lifetime of masking." From childhood, she had been praised for her intelligence but punished, socially and emotionally, for her emotional intensity, need for downtime, and lack of "executive function." Diagnosed with ADHD in her early 30s, Priya felt both relief and quiet grief. She said, "I thought finally I had an explanation and then I felt like I was being handed another label that confirmed I was broken."

In our work together, Priya began the slow process of unlearning internalized ableism. She brought years of language around "not being enough," "being too emotional," and "failing at adulting." Together, we reframed her experiences, not as inadequacies, rather as signals. Her calendar overwhelm wasn't a sign of failure; it was a sign her systems weren't built for her sensory flow. Her difficulty with deadlines wasn't irresponsibility, it was a response to fear and perfectionism, rooted in years of having to overachieve just to be taken seriously.

I introduced her to the idea of *body-trusting productivity*, something I teach often in mentoring, where work is aligned with one's natural rhythms rather than imposed schedules. We integrated "permission-based planning" where Priya began giving herself full permission to work, rest, and create in ways that supported her nervous system.

We also engaged in specific emotional unmasking practices. Priya began journaling in her own words, not professional, not perfect, just *real*. She practiced saying "no" without justification. She started designing meetings at her job that supported different neurotypes. What began as internal healing became a ripple of advocacy for others.

Six months later, Priya shared, "I don't think I've become a new person, I think I've stopped hiding who I always was." This is the power of unlearning ableism: it doesn't make you different. It gives you back to yourself.

## Reflection Questions

1. What beliefs about "normal" or "functional" have you internalized that may no longer serve your truth? Where did they come from?

2. When have you felt the pressure to fix or mask something that was actually a part of your neurodivergent wiring? How did that impact your self-worth?

3. What would it mean to treat your differences as sacred rather than shameful? How would your life shift if you embraced that perspective fully?

4. Who taught you the myth of brokenness, directly or indirectly, and what do you want to say back to that narrative now?

5. What's one step you can take this week to honor your wholeness instead of performing for acceptance?

## PART 4

# RESTORING YOUR INNER WORLD

## CHAPTER 19

# RECLAIMING THE SELF AFTER TRAUMA

Many neurodivergent individuals carry the weight of complex trauma, often rooted in early dysregulation, those countless moments in childhood when your sensitivity, intensity, or needs were dismissed, misunderstood, or shamed. These moments may not have looked like "trauma" from the outside, and yet they created deep fractures within your developing self. When your internal world is repeatedly invalidated, survival becomes the priority. Authenticity becomes a risk.

Reclaiming the self is about recovering access to the sacred parts of yourself that adapted, hid, or went silent to survive. It means gently peeling back the layers of masking, coping, and over-functioning to reconnect with the tender truth underneath. It is not about returning to a mythical "before" some imagined purity untouched by pain.

This reclamation is an act of deep self-loyalty. It involves listening for the quiet voice within that says, *"I'm still here."* It means honoring your inner child who learned to make themselves small to stay safe. It means validating the anger, grief, and longing that arise as sacred invitations to wholeness.

Reconnection happens through presence and permission: permission to grieve what was lost, to feel what was unfelt, and to speak what was once unspeakable. It happens in therapy, in sacred solitude, in art, in movement, in stillness, and often, in the small moments of self-honoring, choosing comfort over performance, authenticity over approval.

To reclaim the self is to come home to the resilient, radiant core of who you are intact, even now. It would be naïve to seek a version of you untouched by harm. This is the beginning of a new story, authored by you, rooted in self-trust and soul-aligned living. You can be free of living in survival mode all the time.

## Meet Leah

Leah had always sensed she was different. From an early age, she lived in a vivid, inner world, an intuitive, deeply feeling child who asked existential questions and found solace in daydreaming. But her emotional intensity didn't fit the emotionally distant culture of her family. Growing up in a household that praised academic achievement and stoicism, Leah quickly learned to mask her intense sensitivities in exchange for approval.

By her teenage years, she had become a master of adaptation, excelling in school, supporting others emotionally, and staying quiet about her own pain. But behind the high achievement lay a growing disconnect from herself. She didn't know how to access her true feelings, only how to "perform" wellness. When friendships become draining or jobs overwhelming, she blamed herself for not being able to "keep up."

In her late 30s, Leah encountered the concept of neurodivergence through a podcast. It felt like a mirror, finally, there was language for her lifelong experience of being "too much" and "not enough" at once. She sought out a therapist trained in trauma-informed care and neurodivergence and began the slow work of reconnecting to her inner world.

Through expressive arts therapy, Leah was invited to paint without purpose. What emerged were recurring images of a little girl in nature, barefoot, curious, quiet. Over time, these images helped Leah meet her inner child with tenderness. She began writing letters to that version of herself, validating the grief of being unseen and the brilliance of her emotional depth.

Reclaiming the self wasn't a single moment it was a series of permissions: to feel, to rest, to be misunderstood without shame. Leah began to share parts of her inner world with close friends, created a ritual of lighting a candle and journaling each evening, and eventually left her corporate job to pursue creative facilitation for other neurodivergent women.

Leah's story is not about fixing but remembering. In healing the rupture between her adult self and her younger self, she reclaimed her voice, her rhythm, and the right to take up space in the world as her whole self.

As we begin to reclaim the self after trauma, we open space for a new way of being one rooted not in constant striving, but in compassionate presence. The journey of healing invites us to soften, to pause, and to tend to the nervous system we once had to override. Rest is not a reward for healing; it is part of healing.

## Reflection Questions

1. In what ways did you adapt or hide parts of yourself in order to feel safe or accepted in childhood?

2. What aspects of your inner world feel the most unfamiliar or neglected today?

3. If you could speak directly to your younger self, what would they need to hear from you right now?

4. What creative or reflective practices help you reconnect with your authentic self?

5. What might self-reclamation look like for you in daily life through boundaries, expression, or rest?

CHAPTER 20

# EMBRACING REST AS RADICAL CARE

For the neurodivergent soul, rest is not optional, it is radical and restorative. In a world that praises productivity, speed, and emotional self-suppression, choosing rest is a revolutionary act of self-loyalty. It interrupts internalized ableism, challenges the myth of endless output, and reaffirms your worth beyond what you do. Rest is not laziness. Rest is wisdom.

This chapter redefines rest as more than sleep or brief moments of downtime. Rest is a *state of being* a return to yourself without the need to perform, fix, or prove. It is the deep exhale after years of holding your breath to survive in environments that misunderstood you. Rest can look like pausing mid-task because your body says, "enough." It can look like daydreaming without guilt, rocking in rhythm, immersing yourself in music, walking slowly through a quiet forest, or lying in a darkened room with your favorite texture nearby.

True rest honors the unique needs of your nervous system. For neurodivergent individuals, this might include intentional solitude to reset overstimulated senses, creating sensory-friendly spaces that calm instead of overwhelming, or engaging in rhythmic, repetitive activities that soothe and regulate, knitting, swaying, drumming, or even sorting objects by color or texture. These are not frivolous, they are medicine.

Rest is also permission. Permission to disconnect from urgency culture. Permission to not respond immediately. Permission to protect your peace. As you begin to view rest as sacred care rather than a reward you must earn, you open a new relationship with your body and soul, one built on trust, rhythm, and respect. You learn to say: *I do not have to burn out to belong. I am allowed to be soft. I am allowed to stop. I am allowed to rest.*

## The 5 Kinds of Rest Necessary for the Neurodivergent Soul

In a world that equates rest with laziness and values hustle over wholeness, the neurodivergent soul often suffers in silence. Many gifted and neurodivergent adults don't even realize they're exhausted until they collapse and complain of being mentally foggy, emotionally brittle, spiritually disoriented. That's because your nervous systems are often operating on overdrive, navigating a world not built for your intense sensitivities, rhythms, or needs.

Rest is not simply sleep or becoming a couch potato. It is a multidimensional practice of repair and re-alignment. For your neurodivergent soul, five kinds of rest are essential forms of medicine not optional luxuries.

### 1. Sensory Rest: Soothing the Overloaded System

For the neurodivergent, the world is often *too loud, too bright, too fast.* Sensory rest is the act of removing stimulation and returning to environments that allow the nervous system to exhale.

This might mean dim lights, noise-canceling headphones, natural textures, a soft blanket, or time spent in nature. Sensory rest isn't passive, it's intentional and tailored. It invites your system back into regulation, where you can actually feel safe *in* your body rather than bracing against it.

**Ask yourself:** When do I feel most calm and internally quiet? What stimuli can I soften or eliminate?

### 2. Cognitive Rest: Releasing the Mental Loop

The gifted mind often never stops thinking, analyzing, solving, revisiting, imagining. Cognitive fatigue builds when we are constantly

"on." Cognitive rest involves giving the brain permission to stop problem-solving. It might come in the form of:
- Doing something repetitive and soothing (like knitting or walking)
- Allowing your thoughts to wander without a goal
- Consuming gentle, non-stimulating media (nature sounds, soft music, slow-paced stories)

It's not about shutting your brain off; it's about shifting it out of performance mode. I often remind my clients: "Even brilliance needs a break. Especially brilliance."

## 3. Emotional Rest: Honoring the Inner Weather
You often experience emotional intensity, feeling the emotional currents of a room, holding others' pain, or cycling through deep inner responses. Emotional rest doesn't mean ignoring your emotions, it means creating space where you don't have to *manage* other people's expectations or reactions.

This might involve time alone, journaling without curation, or being with someone who "gets you" without requiring explanation. Emotional rest allows you to feel what's there without pressure to perform or fix.

Grief, tenderness, and even joy need space to breathe. Without this kind of rest, emotional exhaustion takes root. Emotional rest says: *It's safe to feel, and it's safe to pause.*

## 4. Social Rest: Permission to Be Unmasked
Social fatigue is real, especially when much of your social engagement requires masking, translation, or adaptation. Social rest means being in the presence of others without needing to code-switch or over-explain. Sometimes, it means solitude. Other times, it means kindred company where your presence alone is enough.

Social rest invites you to recalibrate from interactions that drained your energy or required performance. It honors your need to retreat and restore without guilt.

**Ask yourself**: Where do I feel most like myself? Who are the people around whom I can simply be?

## 5. Spiritual Rest: Reconnection with Meaning

Beyond body and mind, your neurodivergent soul needs anchoring in meaning. Spiritual rest is not about religion, it's about reuniting with a sense of sacredness, purpose, or belonging to something larger than yourself.

This may come through meditation, ritual, creative expression, awe in nature, or connection with a divine presence. It's the rest that reminds you that *you are not alone*, and *you are not broken*. It restores your place in the fabric of life and invites your soul to unfold gently.

As I often say in my mentoring practice, "Spiritual rest is when your soul no longer feels exiled from itself."

## Rest Is Revolutionary

For the neurodivergent soul, rest is the restoration of your authenticity. This is a sacred return to your innermost self. It is how you begin to feel like yourself again. Your real rhythms, your true needs, your sacred spark, all show up with more brilliance. When you practice these five kinds of rest, you reclaim your capacity not only to function, but to flourish.

You are meant to live in resonance with your own design. For you, rest is the presence of real restoration. It is how you reconnect with what is most true within your natural rhythm, your real needs, your inner brilliance.

When you allow yourself the gift of true rest, physical, sensory, emotional, creative, and spiritual, you do more than recover from exhaustion. You reawaken your clarity and you rekindle your spark. You remember who you truly are and can once again connect to your inner fire.

Each form of rest is a doorway back to wholeness. With each intentional pause, you honor your unique nervous system. You nourish the parts of you that have been overextended. You create space for inspiration, intuition, and vitality to emerge naturally.

You were never meant to live in constant adaptation or chaos. You were meant to move in harmony with your inner truth. The world may have demanded you bend and shift, and your soul knows the way back to resonance.

In resting, you are coming home. Rest is revolutionary because it defies the lie that your worth is measured by output. It challenges a world that rewards overextension and dismisses sensitivity. When you choose to rest, you reclaim your autonomy. You say, "My energy matters. My needs are valid. My being is enough." For your neurodivergent soul, this is not just healing, it is liberation. In a culture that demands your constant adjustment, rest becomes an act of rebellion and self-respect. It is how you protect your light, restore your clarity, and lead yourself back to the life you were designed to live.

**Rest is Safety**
For the neurodivergent soul, rest is more than restoration, it is safety in motion. It is the body's way of saying, *"I'm no longer in danger."* When we allow ourselves to rest, we are not just slowing down; we are signaling to our nervous systems that it is okay to soften, to release vigilance, to come home.

Many gifted and neurodivergent individuals live in a state of near-constant activation. The world often asks too much of our attention while offering too little understanding in return. Whether it's the executive dysfunction that makes basic tasks feel overwhelming, the sensory overload of navigating loud, unpredictable environments, or the emotional toll of masking and dysregulation, your systems learn to brace. You learn to stay alert, scan for threat, push through even when you are crumbling inside.

In this context, rest becomes synonymous with risk. Slowing down feels unsafe when you've been conditioned to equate stillness with falling behind, softness with weakness, or pausing with failure.

For many, rest has been postponed so long that you forget what it feels like to truly let go.

Yet, healing begins when we redefine rest as a foundational signal of safety. True rest isn't just lying still or being a couch potato. It is the absence of demand. It is the quieting of your internal alarms. It is being in a space, physical or relational, where you don't have to defend, perform, or explain yourself. It is choosing to cocoon when the world feels too sharp and letting yourself emerge only when your body says yes.

For those with trauma histories or intense sensitivity, rest can feel foreign because safety itself has felt conditional. To reclaim rest, then, is to reclaim safety on your own terms. It may start with creating micro-moments of relief like a soft blanket across your shoulders, noise-canceling headphones in a busy space, five minutes alone in your car before walking into a building. These moments add up. They become a language your nervous system learns to trust.

Rest is also relational. Safe rest becomes possible when you surround yourself with people and spaces that don't ask you to be less than you are. Environments where your silence is not misread as disinterest. Where your pacing is not criticized but honored. Where your way of being is not just tolerated but cherished.

Rest teaches your body what safety feels like. Once you have tasted rest, even in small doses, you begin to reorganize your life around it as a sacred agreement with yourself: *I will not abandon my well-being to meet impossible expectations.*

When rest becomes your baseline instead of burnout, you learn to live from a place of wholeness rather than depletion. You learn that you do not need to earn the right to exhale.

Let rest become your sanctuary. Let it remind you that safety is something you can begin to build, breath by breath, choice by choice. Your wait is over.

## Meet Steven

Steven was always praised for his drive. As a child, he balanced honor-roll academics with elite sports, thriving under structure but also never allowed to stop. Rest was synonymous with laziness in his family of origin, and his intense focus and sensory sensitivities went unnoticed in the flurry of expectations.

When Steven hit his late twenties, the structure that had carried him collapsed. He was chronically exhausted, emotionally numb, and unable to sustain full-time work without severe burnout. The diagnosis of autism provided relief, but it also cracked open years of internalized pressure and neglect. He wasn't broken; he was burned out from decades of pushing through.

Discovering the writings of neurodivergent activists reframed rest as something revolutionary not a luxury, but a necessity. For Steven, rest became an act of self-reclamation, a rebellion against the grind culture that had demanded he override his body's signals.

He began with small changes: removing unnecessary stimuli from his environment, using noise-canceling headphones, limiting social obligations. Over time, these evolved into intentional rituals: morning grounding practices with tea and poetry, extended nature walks with no destination, slow movement exercises that honored his body's rhythms.

Most transformative was Steven's redefinition of success. No longer did it mean endless productivity rather it meant alignment. He stopped measuring his worth by deadlines and instead began tracking his energy, creativity, and joy. He built in buffers between tasks, allowed himself to nap guilt-free, and created a "Do Nothing" shelf with books, fidgets, and sensory items to turn to when overwhelmed.

Steven's nervous system, once locked in survival, softened. He reported fewer shutdowns, more emotional clarity, and a deepened spiritual connection. "Rest," he wrote in his journal, "is where I meet myself without masks."

His story reminds us: when the world demands we go faster, choosing your personal pace is a sacred act of resistance and restoration.

As we begin to honor rest as a vital act of care rather than a luxury, we create space not only for physical renewal but for emotional truth to the surface. In that stillness, the voice within, the one we often silence or override, grows louder. Sometimes it speaks with compassion, but more often, it echoes the old narratives we have absorbed from a world that didn't understand us.

## Reflection Questions

1. When in your life have you most associated rest with guilt or weakness? What internalized messages shaped that belief, and are they still serving you?

2. What does your body feel like when it is truly safe? Can you recall a moment, however brief, when you experienced that kind of rest, and what contributed to it?

3. How does your nervous system respond to constant productivity or sensory overload? What signals does it give you when you need to pause but don't feel you can?

4. What might it look like to create more of that space for yourself emotionally, physically, or spiritually?

5. If you believed that rest is not only restorative but revolutionary for your neurodivergent self, what would you change about the rhythm of your days or the expectations you place on yourself?

## CHAPTER 21

# REPAIRING YOUR INNER DIALOGUE

For many neurodivergent individuals, the inner voice is not always a kind one. Over years of being misunderstood, corrected, or shamed, often in subtle, chronic ways a harsh inner dialogue takes root. What begins as external invalidation becomes internalized as self-doubt: *"Why can't I just get it together? What's wrong with me? I should try harder."* These thoughts, often automatic and deeply conditioned, are not reflections of truth. They are echoes of dysregulation and unmet needs.

Repairing your inner dialogue is about relearning how to speak to yourself in your native language of compassion and care. It starts with noticing. Where is your inner voice sharp, punishing, or rushed? Where have you absorbed others' expectations and turned them into self-criticism? What would it sound like to speak to yourself like someone you cherish?

This deep inner work is sacred. It is reparenting. It is inner mentoring. It is choosing to become the safe, steady presence your younger self always needed. It might sound like: It's okay to need a break. You don't have to explain your feelings of overwhelm. You are not behind; your rhythm is valid.

Repair often begins in micro-moments. A gentle hand on your heart when the critic rises. A pause after a mistake where you say, I'm learning. Rewriting your inner dialogue is about allowing love to have a voice too rather than silencing your fear.

When your internal landscape becomes a sanctuary instead of a battlefield, everything shifts. Your nervous system relaxes. Your relationships deepen. And most importantly, you begin to trust your own presence again. You become a place where your soul feels safe to land.

As you begin to repair our inner dialogue, you create a more compassionate and affirming relationship with yourself. Healing the way you speak to yourself is only one part of the journey. Your environment, the spaces you live, work, and rest also speak to your nervous systems in powerful ways. Just as words shape your inner world, sensory experiences shape your felt sense of safety, comfort, and regulation. The next step is learning to create physical spaces that support who you are at a core level.

**Meet Eli**

Eli is a gifted person who is an emotionally perceptive adult in his early 50s who has spent most of his life navigating a punishing internal monologue. From childhood, he had been labeled "overly dramatic" and "too sensitive" by teachers and caregivers who didn't understand his deep processing and emotional intensity. Though he excelled academically and professionally, his inner world was a battlefield, a relentless chorus of self-doubt, perfectionism, and quiet despair.

When Eli was diagnosed with complex PTSD and later identified as autistic, the revelations were equal parts liberating and devastating. Suddenly, the harsh inner voice that had driven him to succeed at all costs was exposed for what it was: an inherited voice, born of survival, not truth.

With the support of a neuro affirming therapist and mentoring with me, Eli began to explore parts work and inner dialogue exercises. At first, the idea of speaking to "parts" of himself felt awkward. But as he began naming these parts, the Critic, the Protector, the Silent Child, he realized how much of his energy had gone toward silencing them rather than listening to what they needed.

The silent child within carried the grief of never being comforted when overwhelmed. In one session, Eli broke down in tears as he imagined holding that younger version of himself, not fixing or analyzing him, but simply saying: "You didn't do anything wrong. You were just feeling too much, too fast, in a world that didn't know what to do with you."

He created affirmations that felt authentic and rooted in truth. "I am allowed to rest.", "My emotions are wise.", "I do not have to earn safety." Eli also used voice recordings, speaking to himself in the tone he never received as a child. Listening to his own voice, gentle and affirming, became a nightly ritual.

Over time, the critic softened. It didn't disappear, but it lost its authority. What grew in its place was a compassionate witness, the voice of his authentic self, no longer at war with himself.

Eli's story is one of quiet revolution: changing not what he did, but how he spoke to himself. He reclaimed his inner space, not by silencing his parts, but by befriending them.

## Reflection Questions

1. What are some common phrases or thoughts your inner critic uses? Where do you think those messages originally came from?

2. How does your inner dialogue shift depending on your environment, sensory state, or level of fatigue?

3. When was the last time you spoke to yourself with true gentleness? What did it feel like?

4. If your inner voice reflected the tone of someone who truly understood and loved your neurodivergent self, what would it say to you today?

5. What small daily practice could you introduce to begin softening and reshaping the way you speak to yourself?

CHAPTER 22

# SENSORY SANCTUARIES: CREATING SPACES THAT SOOTHE

Many neurodivergent people live partially or fully disembodied, disconnected from the body due to overwhelm, hypersensitivity, or trauma. This section invites you back into your sensory and somatic experience, not as something to "fix," but as a portal to healing.

For the neurodivergent soul, the world can often feel too loud, too bright, too fast, or simply *too much*. From flickering fluorescent lights to scratchy fabrics, crowded spaces, and subtle but constant noise, modern life assaults the senses in ways that can be invisible to others but deeply disruptive to us. When this overstimulation becomes chronic, we don't just get irritated, we begin to disconnect. We disembody.

We'll explore embodiment practices such as breathwork, gentle movement, creative arts, and sensory tuning, each personalized to meet the body with respect and responsiveness. Sensory profiles are presented not as diagnostic tools, but as keys to understanding how the body communicates needs and preferences.

**Recognizing Disembodiment**
Disembodiment is the soul's protective strategy when the body becomes an uncomfortable or unsafe place to inhabit. You may be disembodied if you:

- Often feel "floaty" or not quite present in your body
- Forget to eat, drink, or use the bathroom for long periods
- Struggle to notice internal signals like hunger, fatigue, or pain
- Feel emotionally numb or overly reactive
- Experience a sense of detachment or operating on autopilot
- Spend most of your energy "in your head," problem-solving, analyzing, or retreating into thought loops.

These are not failures. They are adaptations, your body's way of saying, "This doesn't feel safe". Reconnection begins with gentleness and is free of judgment.

## Why Sensory Sanctuary Matters

While many conversations around neurodivergence focus on coping strategies, few address the healing power of creating environments that actually honor your sensory reality. A sensory sanctuary is more than a tidy room or a place to escape, it is a sacred space where your nervous system is invited to rest, restore, and recalibrate. It communicates: *You belong here. Your needs matter here. You can soften here.*

When your outer environment reflects and respects your inner world, your body begins to trust again. You drop back into yourself. You come home to your authentic nature.

## Building Your Personal Sanctuary

Creating a sensory sanctuary doesn't require perfection or expensive materials. It begins with awareness and intention. Ask yourself:
- What environments make me feel safe, grounded, and soothed?
- Which textures, colors, and sounds comfort me, and which ones agitate me?
- Where in my current space do I feel most able to exhale? How can I expand on that feeling?

Start small. Maybe it's a corner with soft lighting and a blanket. A weighted item on your lap while you work. A curated playlist that grounds your mind. Scented oils that evoke calm. A texture that signals safety. These are not indulgences. They are access points to regulation.

I often say in her mentoring work, "Healing is not just about what you do, it's also about where you are and how that space holds you." Your space can become a partner in your healing, a container for your transformation.

### Daily Practices of Sensory Stewardship

- **Create a "reset ritual"** at the end of each day, a way to signal to your nervous system that you can unwind now. This could be dimming lights, playing soft music, stretching, or changing into comfortable clothing.
- **Designate a "soft zone"** in your home or office that includes at least one sensory element you love. Return to it often.
- **Use intentional sensory cues** to shift state. Smells (lavender, vanilla), sounds (wind chimes, ocean waves), or weighted pressure can help transition you from alert to at ease.
- **Keep your space responsive** to your sensory needs. What soothes you one week may change the next week. This is totally expected as you grow and heal. Allow your sanctuary to evolve with you.

### Coming Home to Yourself

The journey of healing is not linear. It weaves through the body, the mind, and the spaces we inhabit. Sensory sanctuaries are not just about peace, they're about presence. They allow you to reclaim your right to *feel safe being you*, fully and unapologetically.

When you stop forcing your body to adapt to the world and instead allow the world around you to reflect your true sensory needs, you begin to return to yourself. You land in your own skin. You breathe more fully. You listen more deeply.

And slowly, beautifully, you remember: *This body is mine. This life is mine. I can choose what surrounds me.*

## Meet Jennifer

Jennifer is a late-diagnosed ADHD and autistic woman in her mid-30s who spent most of her life living from the neck up, thinking, analyzing, and overprocessing. The world was loud, bright, fast, and unrelenting, and the only way she'd learned to survive was to disconnect from her body. It felt like a foreign country at times too much, at times completely numb.

As a child, Jennifer loved to twirl in circles, sing to herself, and lie under trees for hours. But by adolescence, these soothing rituals were replaced by tension: rigid posture, clenched jaw, and holding her breath without realizing it. "Stillness made me feel exposed," she later said. "Movement was only safe when it had a purpose."

After a significant period of burnout, she joined a neurodivergent-led somatic group which led her to mentoring designed for neurodivergent adults. She encountered the idea that embodiment didn't have to be dramatic or performative. It could be subtle, gentle, and on her terms.

She started with micro-movements: wiggling her fingers, tapping her feet, rolling her shoulders, movements that reintroduced her to sensation without overwhelm. She discovered she loved slow, rhythmic movement, especially when paired with soft music or drumming. Dancing alone in her room with dim lighting became a nightly ritual, no formal steps, no choreography, just presence.

Jennifer also began exploring sensory profiling, not as a diagnostic checklist, but as a way to understand how her body communicated. She realized she was sensory-seeking in touch but sensory-avoidant with sound. She adapted her environment to accommodate her nervous system needs: soft blankets, textured clothing, noise-dampening curtains, and essential oils for grounding.

One of the most powerful shifts came when she began dialoguing with her body as if it were a friend. "What do you need today?" she would ask. And often, the answer was silence, stillness, or play. Through this slow reconnection, Jennifer discovered that her body wasn't the enemy after all, it had been protecting her all along. By listening, rather than overriding, she cultivated not just sensory peace, but deep self-trust. Her story reminds us that healing doesn't require grand gestures; it begins with returning to the body as sacred space.

As you begin to shape spaces that honor your sensory truth, you may notice something unexpected: your inner world starts to quiet. In that calm, a deeper need often emerges, the need to slow down. For the neurodivergent soul, life is often lived in fast-forward or under pressure to keep pace with systems that move too fast, too loud, too chaotically. Sensory sanctuaries offer the *where* but slowing down offers the *how*.

## Sensory Sanctuaries: Creating Spaces That Soothe

**Reflection Questions**

1. What are three sensory experiences that consistently soothe you and how can you invite them into your daily space?

2. How do you know when you're becoming disembodied or disconnected from your body? What signals do you overlook or minimize?

3. What environments from your past (a room, a place in nature, a person's home) made you feel safe in your body? What qualities did they have?

4. What sensory triggers do you regularly tolerate that could be softened or eliminated?

5. How can you begin to treat your sensory preferences not as quirks, but as sacred guidance?

## CHAPTER 23

# THE ART OF SLOWING DOWN

In the rhythm of modern life, slowing down can feel like an act of rebellion. The world around us pulses with urgency, deadlines, notifications, expectations. For neurodivergent souls, this external pressure collides painfully with internal experiences. The gifted mind races with ideas, the ADHD spirit craves novelty yet struggles with overwhelm, the autistic nervous system senses every detail with acute intensity.

Yet, paradoxically, this rush often leads not to clarity but to chaos; not to accomplishment but to exhaustion. The art of slowing down is not merely about pausing. It is a radical practice of listening deeply to your body, to your emotions, to your soul's subtle rhythms.

To slow down is to reclaim your presence in a world that constantly demands your absence. It is to create sacred space for intuition, creativity, and healing. It is to honor the natural tempo of your neurodivergent mind and body rather than forcing them into a mold of speed and efficiency.

Slowing down reveals the hidden currents beneath the surface of your daily life, the anxiety beneath the busyness, the exhaustion beneath the achievement, the longing beneath the distraction. When you slow down, you open a doorway back to yourself.

This practice does not come easily. It often requires permission from your environment, from your responsibilities, and most importantly, from yourself. It demands courage to resist the cultural narrative that equates speed with worth and stillness with laziness.

Yet those who embrace the art of slowing down discover that true productivity is born from presence, not pressure. Insight blossoms in the quiet spaces. Connection deepens when we show up fully, not hurriedly.

### Meet Samuel

Samuel is a 32-year-old autistic and ADHD man who had long been caught in a whirlwind of activity. An entrepreneur in the tech world, his mind was a constant storm of ideas, plans, and "what ifs." His days were packed with back-to-back meetings, endless to-do lists, and a relentless drive to "keep up."

Despite his outward success, Samuel felt perpetually drained, disconnected, and anxious. He described his experience as "trying to run a marathon on a treadmill that never stops." He struggled to sustain focus, often jumping from one task to another without completion, overwhelmed by sensory input and internal restlessness.

When Samuel began mentoring services with me, one of my first invitations was to explore the possibility of slowing down. This was unfamiliar and uncomfortable, slowing down felt like falling behind or worse, being lazy.

Together, we worked on practices tailored to Samuel's unique neurodivergent rhythms:

- **Mindful pauses**: Samuel began integrating brief moments of stillness into his day, five minutes of focused breathing or noticing sensory details around him.
- **Sensory awareness**: He learned to recognize early signs of overwhelm and use slowing down as a way to prevent escalation.
- **Reframing productivity**: Samuel shifted his mindset from "doing more" to "being more present," recognizing that presence often led to clearer, more creative outcomes.
- **Creating rhythm**: Rather than fighting against his fluctuating

energy levels, Samuel structured his workday around periods of high focus followed by deliberate rest.

Over time, Samuel noticed a profound change: his anxiety decreased, his creativity deepened, and his connection to himself strengthened. He no longer viewed slowing down as a weakness but as an essential act of self-care and empowerment.

Slowing down is not simply a pause, it is an invitation to reclaim your soul's tempo, to dance with the natural cadence of your mind and body. In a world that is rushing past your gift is to be the still point, the sacred space where true healing and growth unfold.

Slowing down is an act of profound courage and deep self-respect. It invites you to step off the endless treadmill of rushing and striving, and instead, step into the richness of your own experience. As you cultivate presence, you create fertile ground for clarity, creativity, and connection to flourish. Remember, your worth is not measured by speed or output, but by the fullness with which you live your moments, slow or fast, quiet or loud, all of it belongs to your beautifully neurodivergent soul.

**Reflection Questions**

1. What emotions or thoughts arise in you when you choose to slow down? Are they rooted in your own truth, or in external expectations you've internalized?

2. How does your neurodivergent mind respond when you create space for stillness and quiet? What do you begin to notice that was previously hidden beneath the noise?

3. Where in your daily life do you feel most rushed or pulled away from yourself? What might it look like to reclaim even a small part of that time for intentional slowing?

4. What internal or external messages tell you that slowing down is unsafe, unproductive, or selfish? How would your life change if you no longer believed those messages?

5. When have you experienced clarity, insight, or emotional relief by slowing down? How can you create more sacred pauses like that, woven gently into your rhythm of living?

## CHAPTER 24

# RITUALS FOR REGULATION

Structure can be a double-edged sword for the neurodivergent soul. On one hand, routines can create safety, predictability, and calm. On the other hand, rigid schedules often collapse under the weight of sensory overwhelm, executive function challenges, emotional depth, and real-life chaos. For many gifted and neurodivergent adults, traditional structure simply doesn't hold. That's where *ritual* enters.

Unlike rigid routines, rituals are flexible, soulful, and embodied. They anchor us not to productivity, but to presence. They don't demand perfection or consistency, they offer a touchstone. Even when the day spins out, even when everything feels disorganized, a small ritual can regulate the nervous system, restore a sense of center, and reconnect us to the sacred within the ordinary.

Whether you are someone who finds comfort in traditional faith or someone who forges your own spiritual path, rituals can bridge the inner and outer worlds. They help us *reclaim rhythm*, even when we can't create routine.

**Why Regulation Matters**
The nervous system is the gateway to our ability to think, feel, connect, and create. When we are dysregulated, hyperaroused, shut down, or scattered, our access to clarity, connection, and creativity diminishes. For the neurodivergent, this dysregulation often happens quickly and silently. The body goes into overdrive, and unless we have tools, we may not realize it until we're deep into exhaustion or reactivity.

Rituals help regulate by creating micro-moments of safety.

They cue the body that it's okay to soften. To come back online. To come home.

Let's explore both common and lesser-known rituals that support regulation.

## Common (and Highly Effective) Regulation Rituals
1. **Breathwork or Simple Breath Cues.** Noticing the inhale and extending the exhale signals safety to the brain. Try "box breathing" (inhale-4, hold-4, exhale-4, hold-4) or a calming sigh with vocal tone.
2. **Walking or Gentle Movement.** Rhythmic walking, rocking, or stretching helps the nervous system discharge adrenaline. Even 5 minutes can reset your system.
3. **Prayer and Inner Stillness.** For many, a quiet morning prayer, reading from a sacred text, or sitting in silence becomes a centering ritual. Whether in a religious or spiritual context, this intentional pause roots the soul.
4. **Music with Intention.** A favorite song that grounds you. A playlist for different moods. A sacred chant or hymn. Sound has regulatory power, use it consciously.
5. **Drinking Something Warm.** Tea, coffee, or bone broth, sipped slowly, with presence, can act as an anchoring ritual. It's not about caffeine or nutrition, it's about grounding.

## Lesser Known (and Powerful) Rituals for Your Neurodivergent Soul

**Weight and Pressure Rituals** - Using a weighted blanket, applying gentle pressure to joints, or wrapping in a heavy shawl before a difficult task can regulate sensory input.

**Layered Texture Rituals** - Wearing certain fabrics, keeping a stone in your pocket, or stroking a textured item mindfully can offer both sensory and emotional grounding.

**"Transition Touchstones"** - Keep a small object (like a smooth stone or essential oil roller) at doorways or desks. Touch it during transitions as a cue to breathe and center.

**Time-Awareness Anchors** - Use hourly chimes, prayer bells, or recurring phone reminders to return to your body throughout the day. Not to be productive, but to be present.

**Self-Dialogue or "Soul Check-In"** - Take one minute to ask: *"How am I, really?"* and write down one sentence. This creates a connection between your conscious self and deeper soul needs.

**Regulation Through Creativity** - Engaging in 10 minutes of doodling, free-writing, or singing a single verse of a song can re-regulate the nervous system through non-verbal release.

## Meet Timothy

Timothy is a 50-year-old military veteran and gifted thinker who came to mentoring carrying both high achievement and chronic inner agitation. "I don't sit still well," he said. "I hate schedules, but I know I need something. My mind's always on fire."

As we worked together, it became clear that Timothy didn't need a strict morning routine, he needed regulation rituals that honored his wiring. We co-created a list of "floating rituals" that he could pick from based on how his body and mind felt each morning. Some days it was five minutes of standing barefoot on the porch with coffee. Other days, it was tapping his chest while repeating an affirmation or doing 10 pushups to shift energy.

He also began marking the end of his workday with a ritual of lighting a candle and speaking out loud one thing he was proud of and one thing he was releasing. Over time, he stopped framing his day as "on track or off track" and began measuring it by one question: "Did I return to myself today?"

Timothy told me, "These rituals don't demand anything of me. They are an invitation for me. That's what I needed, an invitation home."

## Reflection Questions

1. What daily activities already bring you a sense of calm, focus, or connection can any of these become intentional rituals?

2. When you feel dysregulated, what sensations do you notice in your body? What ritual could meet that moment with compassion?

3. What spiritual or grounding practices from your upbringing or culture might be reclaimed or reshaped to support your current nervous system?

4. How does your relationship with structure or routine affect your ability to care for yourself? Where could rituals offer more flexible support?

5. If you gave yourself permission to create your own soul-nourishing rituals without needing anyone's approval, what would one look like?

## CHAPTER 25

# CREATIVITY AS SELF-SOOTHING

Creativity is often celebrated as a means to produce, to innovate, to perform. But for the neurodivergent soul, creativity holds an even deeper power. It is a vital form of self-soothing, a language through which the restless mind and overwhelmed heart find rest and expression.

When the world feels too loud, too fast, or too demanding, creative acts can become a refuge. Whether it's painting, writing, crafting, music, or movement, creativity offers a way to slow the internal noise and reconnect with the self. It is not about the final product or the approval of others; it's about the process, the gentle unfolding of inner experience into form.

For many neurodivergent individuals, creativity bypasses cognitive overwhelm and taps directly into emotional regulation and healing. It transforms anxiety into rhythm, chaos into pattern, intensity into beauty. In this way, creativity becomes a balm for the nervous system and a bridge back to wholeness.

In a society focused on productivity, creativity as self-soothing is often misunderstood or undervalued. When art is only recognized if it is "good enough" or "marketable," the sacred act of creation risks becoming another source of pressure. The challenge, then, is to reclaim creativity as a healing practice, a loving dialogue with your own soul.

## Meet Sofia

Sofia is a 29-year-old woman who shared that she has been diagnosed with ADHD and giftedness who discovered early on that her mind was a storm of ideas and emotions that could be difficult to navigate. School often felt suffocating, the rigid structures and constant demand for "correct" answers left her anxious and restless.

In adulthood, Sofia turned to creativity as a lifeline. She began journaling and creating collages, not with any goal of perfection or audience, but simply as a way to express what words alone couldn't hold. These moments became sacred spaces where she could sit with her feelings, untangle overwhelming thoughts, and soothe her racing mind.

During her mentoring sessions with me, Sofia explored how to deepen this creative self-care:

- **Permission to create without judgment:** Sofia learned to let go of the pressure to "make something good" and embraced the freedom to create messy, imperfect art.
- **Using creativity to regulate emotions:** When anxiety peaked, Sofia practiced returning to her journal or collage supplies to channel that energy safely.
- **Recognizing creative blocks as signals:** Rather than forcing herself when stuck, Sofia began to listen deeply to what her resistance was telling her about her needs.
- **Integrating creativity into daily routines:** She carved out regular time for these practices, not as chores, but as nourishing rituals.

Over time, Sofia's creative practice transformed from a private refuge into a vibrant source of resilience. She reported feeling more grounded, less reactive to stress, and more connected to her inner world. The act of making became a mirror reflecting her inherent worth and the vibrant complexity of her neurodivergent soul.

Creativity is a self-soothing radical act of kindness toward yourself. You step into a compassionate, playful relationship with your inner world. It invites you to meet your inner self with curiosity and compassion, transforming overwhelm into expression and isolation into connection. By nurturing this sacred practice, you open a doorway to healing that honors your neurodivergent soul's depth and resilience. Remember, beauty lies in the loving process of creation itself.

## Reflection Questions

1. How do I currently experience creativity such as performance, pressure, or healing?

2. In what ways can I give myself permission to create simply for the sake of soothing and expression?

3. What small creative practices could I incorporate into my life to support emotional regulation and self-connection?

4. What creative expressions in the past have brought me a sense of calm, grounding, or joy and how might I revisit them now?

5. How can I redefine creativity on my own terms, free from comparison, productivity, or perfectionism?

CHAPTER 26

# WHAT RESISTANCE SAYS ABOUT YOUR NEEDS

We often treat resistance like a problem to eliminate. We push against it, shame ourselves for it, try to outsmart or override it. In a world that celebrates hustle and output, resistance is seen as weakness, laziness, or failure to "follow through." But what if resistance is not your enemy? What if it's a form of inner communication, one of the few ways your nervous system or inner self knows how to get your attention?

For the neurodivergent soul, resistance frequently appears where there is a mismatch between **what is being asked of you** and **what your system truly needs**. It is not merely procrastination or avoidance. It can be a signal of sensory overload, emotional dysregulation, moral incongruence, or the exhaustion of masking. It may arise in response to an unkind tone, a rigid expectation, a looming deadline that ignores your energy rhythms.

Resistance, in its purest form, is intelligence. It is your body saying, "*Something isn't right.*" It is your intuition saying, "*This isn't aligned.*" It is your nervous system saying, "*I don't feel safe enough to proceed.*"

Unfortunately, many of us have been taught to override these signals. To comply. To push through. To numb. This creates an internal war: a part of you pushing to meet the external demand, and another part digging in its heels, pleading to be heard.

Rather than judge resistance, you can learn to listen to what it is trying to tell you. We can ask questions instead of issuing orders:

- What am I truly afraid of here?
- What part of this task or interaction feels unsafe or overwhelming?
- Is your resistance rooted in perfectionism, or does something deeper need to be addressed?

Sometimes, resistance means you need rest before you engage. Sometimes, it means you need reassurance, structure, or clarity. And sometimes, resistance means you're walking someone else's path, not your own.

For gifted and neurodivergent individuals, resistance often shows up around things we deeply care about. That paradox can be painful feeling stuck even when something truly matters. But that very tension is a doorway. It means there's something sacred there, waiting to be approached with care and understanding, not force.

When you stop interpreting resistance as failure, it can become a trusted guide. You can meet it with curiosity: What are you trying to tell me? What are you protecting me from? What do I need to feel supported in this?

When met with compassion, resistance becomes a bridge rather than a blockade. It connects you back to your truth.

## Meet Elijah

Elijah is a gifted 43-year-old man with ADHD who had spent much of his adult life launching ambitious projects—and abandoning them. Each time he set a new goal, he'd start with intense enthusiasm, only to find himself procrastinating, feeling paralyzed, or veering off into unrelated tangents. He called it self-sabotage. Others called him flaky. Inside, he felt ashamed and confused. Why couldn't he "just do it," especially when he knew he was capable?

When Elijah began working with a mentor who understood neurodivergence, he started looking at his resistance not as sabotage, but as signal. Together, they unpacked the patterns:

- He resisted tasks when they lacked meaning or personal resonance.

- He felt blocked when his schedule was too rigid or lacked novelty.
- He froze when he feared his work wouldn't meet impossibly high standards.

Most importantly, Elijah realized that he had internalized the belief that his brain was "too much", too scattered, too passionate, too unpredictable. He had been trying to fit himself into systems and timelines that were never built for him.

With this insight, Elijah changed his approach. He began building his days around rhythms rather than strict schedules. He added more movement and music to his work sessions. He practiced naming his needs without apologizing, and he allowed himself to rest when the resistance signaled overload rather than laziness.

Over time, Elijah no longer feared his resistance. He used it as a barometer, checking in when it arose and adjusting instead of forcing. As his self-trust grew, so did his ability to follow through on his terms.

**Reflection Questions**

1. When you feel resistance in your body or mind, what is your first reaction? Do you tend to push through, withdraw, or criticize yourself?

2. Think of a recent moment when you felt strong resistance. What might that resistance have been trying to protect you from or alert you to?

3. What patterns do you notice about when and where resistance shows up in your life? What do those patterns reveal about your needs?

4. How would your relationship with resistance change if you saw it as wisdom rather than weakness? What new choices might become possible?

5. What support, environment, or inner permission do you need to meet your resistance with compassion and curiosity rather than shame?

CHAPTER 27

# BUILDING A SAFE INNER SANCTUARY

Your inner sanctuary is real. It is the sacred space within you where your nervous system settles, your inner knowing rises, and your soul breathes freely. It exists not as a fantasy, but as a felt truth, one you can shape, nourish, and return to at any time. For you, as a neurodivergent being who may have long felt emotionally unanchored or energetically displaced, building this sanctuary is an act of devotion. It is how you reclaim inner ground.

You deserve a place within that is entirely untouched by judgment, unaffected by the world's demands. This sanctuary is a place of profound safety, not constructed from fear, but rooted in belonging. It reflects the textures, symbols, and energies that feel like home to you. Whether you access it through visualization, meditative imagery, or quiet ritual, it becomes a living space for rest, clarity, and self-connection.

Building this space begins with intention. You begin by choosing to honor your inner world as worthy of beauty and reverence. Through practices like guided imagery, sensory grounding, spiritual anchoring, and symbolic rituals, you begin to shape an internal refuge that supports your unique rhythm. Every time you visit this place, whether in silence, breath, prayer, or imagination you strengthen your capacity to self-regulate, to feel safe in your own presence, and to trust your own inner compass.

This sanctuary is not only a retreat in times of distress. It is also a generative space, a place from which your truth can speak clearly, your intuition can unfold, and your creativity can rise. It holds the sacred memory of who you are when all masks are set down and all external noise fades.

Living from this space allows you to meet the world from your center. It allows you to make decisions from clarity rather than fear, to connect without losing yourself, and to rest without guilt. Your sanctuary becomes the foundation from which your healing deepens, and your life expands.

You are allowed to have a space that honors your design. You are allowed to come home to yourself fully and without apology. This inner sanctuary is not something you must earn; it is your birthright. And every moment you tend to it, you affirm your worth, your wisdom, and your wholeness.

## Meet Jonas

Jonas is a twice exceptional (2e) adult in his late 20s who had long felt emotionally untethered. Growing up, he was identified as gifted early on yet frequently punished for "spacing out" or withdrawing. He wasn't being defiant, he was dissociating, escaping the constant sensory and emotional barrage that overwhelmed his system. His intelligence was praised, but his anxiety and quiet intuition were pathologized.

By adulthood, Jonas was successful on the outside but fractured within. He had learned how to code-switch to survive mirroring others in social situations, concealing his anxiety, suppressing his intuitive perceptions. But he felt emotionally homeless. Therapy helped him unpack his masking and trauma, but what lingered was a persistent sense of inner dislocation.

It was during a guided visualization exercise in a neurodivergent-affirming support group that Jonas was first introduced to the concept of an inner sanctuary, a space inside himself, created not from memory or fantasy, but from deep knowing.

At first, his sanctuary was hard to access. His mind raced, trying to "build it right." But his facilitator encouraged slowness. Over time, through visualization, breathwork, and sensory anchoring, a consistent inner landscape emerged: a quiet forest clearing, with mossy ground and a small cabin filled with books and light. It wasn't a memory; it was something deeper. It felt safe.

He returned to this space daily, even if only for moments. He added ritual: lighting a candle before visiting, journaling afterward, and drawing images from the space. It became a refuge, not to escape reality, but to reconnect with it more rooted and resourced.

Jonas began to decorate his physical space with items that reflected his sanctuary, soft textures, earth tones, gentle lighting. Over time, this bridging between inner and outer space deepened his sense of belonging. His inner world was no longer hidden or fragmented, it was honored, inhabited, and alive.

He often described his sanctuary not as a fantasy, but as "a map back to myself." In moments of dysregulation, anxiety, or despair, returning to that inner clearing gave him a felt sense of being held.

Jonas's story teaches us that the safe space we long for is not always something we must find in the world, it can be something we build within, with care, imagination, and intention.

**Reflection Questions:**

1. What qualities help me feel deeply safe, soothed, and fully myself and how can I weave those into my inner sanctuary?

2. When I imagine a space within me that feels sacred and peaceful, what colors, textures, symbols, or elements appear?

3. How can I regularly access this inner space to support my emotional regulation and sense of rootedness?

4. What spiritual, sensory, or creative practices help me anchor into my own energy and truth?

5. In what ways can I honor and protect the sacredness of my inner world in my daily life?

## PART 5

# PURPOSE WITHOUT BURNOUT

# CHAPTER 28

# THE PRESSURE TO BE EXTRAORDINARY

For many gifted and neurodivergent individuals, the pressure to be extraordinary begins early, sometimes before they even understand what that word means. The moment a child is labeled as "bright," "advanced," "talented," or "special," a silent contract begins to form: *You must live up to the potential we see in you.* What starts as recognition quickly becomes expectation.

Instead of being allowed to *be*, many of us learn to *perform*. We learn that love and praise are linked to achievement. That our worth is tied to how well we impress, produce, or outshine. That the only way to feel safe or valuable is to be exceptional.

But here's the paradox: being gifted and neurodivergent doesn't always mean being high-achieving in the traditional sense. In fact, many of us experience nonlinear paths, bursts of brilliance alongside burnout, and periods of deep inner growth that don't look like external success. And when the world measures us by narrow standards, grades, accolades, career status, we are often misjudged, and worse, we begin to misjudge ourselves.

In my mentoring work with neurodivergent adults, I hear it often: *"I was supposed to do something amazing, and I feel like I've failed."* But what if the pressure to be extraordinary is part of the problem? What if your soul is not here to perform, but to evolve?

### The Hidden Cost of Exceptionality

The gifted neurodivergent soul often carries the weight of unspoken contracts:

- If I'm not ahead, I'm falling behind.
- If I don't live up to my potential, I'm wasting my life.
- If I stop achieving, I'll disappear.

This pressure leads to chronic anxiety, perfectionism, imposter syndrome, and deep emotional fatigue. We begin to fear rest, because rest feels like falling short. We fear saying "I don't know," because it might tarnish the identity we've been taught to maintain.

Over time, this leads to a disconnection from authentic self-expression. The soul becomes trapped in a performance loop, constantly asking: Am I doing enough? Am I impressing others enough? Am I exceptional enough to be safe, loved, or worthy?

Being neurodivergent means your path will never look like the mainstream. Your creativity may not thrive on demand. Your progress may not be linear. And your greatness may not come in the form of external achievement, but in your presence, insight, integrity, or healing.

My work reminds you that real fulfillment is not found in chasing gold stars, but in living in alignment with our inner brilliance. *"You are not here to be impressive. You are here to be fully alive."* This shift from performance to presence is at the heart of reclaiming your life.

### Meet Evan

Evan is a 39-year-old client who called for mentoring services, feeling exhausted and ashamed. As a child, he had been identified as gifted and spent much of his youth praised for his advanced vocabulary, creativity, and academic success. "They all said I'd do something big," he told me. "But I'm working a quiet job, struggling with executive functioning, and I feel like I've let everyone down."

As we worked together, it became clear that Evan's sense of failure wasn't rooted in actual failure but in a relentless inner narrative shaped by early expectations. He was comparing his life not to his own values or desires, but to a projected version of himself that had never accounted for his neurodivergence, his sensitivity, or his authentic pace.

Through intentional mentoring, Evan began to explore what "extraordinary" really meant to him not his parents, not teachers, not society. He realized that the work he was doing supporting teens with learning differences was in fact deeply meaningful. He reconnected with his creative writing practice, not for publication or praise, but because it helped him feel alive. In releasing the pressure to prove himself, Evan rediscovered who he actually was. His story is a reminder: the soul's success is measured in alignment, not applause.

Your soul doesn't thrive under pressure; it thrives in presence. And the antidote to the relentless drive to prove yourself is not in doing more, but in *slowing down*. In the next chapter, we'll explore how embracing a slower, more soul-aligned pace isn't a sign of weakness or failure, but a return to your natural rhythm. When we slow down, we stop reacting and start listening. This is where healing begins, and where a different kind of extraordinary unfolds.

## Reflection Questions

1. When did you first feel the pressure to be "extraordinary" or different in a way that needed to be proven?

2. What beliefs have you internalized about achievement and worth and where did they come from?

3. In what ways has the drive to be impressive disconnected you from your own values, needs, or desires?

4. What might "extraordinary" look like if defined by your soul not society?

5. How would your life change if you no longer had to earn your worth through achievement?

## CHAPTER 29

# RETHINKING PRODUCTIVITY AND WORTH

From an early age, many of us were taught that our value lies in what we do, not in who we are. Praise came when we achieved. Acceptance came when we performed. Love was easier to access when we were "productive" in ways the world could easily measure. And for the gifted and neurodivergent soul, this message becomes a double bind: our intensity, creativity, and depth are often only welcomed when they produce visible, tangible results that others understand. What if your worth has nothing to do with productivity?

Let that land for a moment. Your worth is not a function of how many tasks you complete, how well you manage your to-do list, or how "on top of things" you appear. Your worth is intrinsic, unchanging, unconditional, and rooted in your being, not your output.

The neurodivergent mind often doesn't follow linear patterns of work. Bursts of energy may come at strange hours. Deep focus might appear during times others are winding down. You might do nothing for days and then create something brilliant in a single afternoon. This rhythm is not broken. It is simply *different*. But in a culture that idolizes grind, hustle, and visible productivity, it's easy to feel like you're falling short. That something is wrong with *you* when, in truth, the system never made space for your natural rhythm to begin with.

## The Myth of Constant Output

The myth that productivity equals worth is deeply embedded in our culture. We're taught to measure success in units: emails answered, goals achieved, money earned. Even rest is often justified only if it leads to "greater performance later." The neurodivergent person, who may experience executive functioning challenges, sensory overload, and non-linear energy cycles, often internalizes this myth in painful ways.

You may have said to yourself:
- "I didn't get enough done today, so I'm behind."
- "I wasted this day; I didn't accomplish anything."
- "I need to push harder to prove I'm not lazy or broken."

These narratives aren't just exhausting, they're harmful. They strip you of the right to exist outside of doing. They keep your nervous system in a chronic state of fight-or-flight. And they disconnect you from the joy, wonder, and meaning that come from simply being.

## Reclaiming Inner Rhythms

Rethinking productivity is not about becoming less ambitious. It's about redefining success in a way that honors your body, your energy, and your soul's pace.

What if productivity looked like:
- Resting when your body asks—not when the calendar says it's allowed?
- Spending time deep in thought or imagination without needing a tangible result?
- Saying no to things that deplete you, even if they look "productive" on the outside?
- Creating, connecting, or healing in ways that don't produce income or accolades, but bring peace to your inner world?

In my mentoring work, I often help clients untangle the pressure to "perform wellness" and instead guide them toward *embodied alignment*. This means honoring your nervous system, embracing your natural energy cycles, and measuring success by how connected you feel to yourself, not how much you got done.

## Soul-Aligned Productivity

There is such a thing as soul-aligned productivity. It doesn't ignore the reality of responsibilities, but it moves from intention rather than compulsion. It listens before it acts. It honors rest as a form of preparation. It sees slowness not as slacking, but as strategy.

When you shift from urgency to presence, productivity becomes a *byproduct* of alignment, not a performance for validation.

Ask yourself:
- Is this task an act of obligation or expression?
- Am I honoring my capacity or pushing past it out of fear?
- What would feel nourishing rather than draining right now?

Let this reframe seep into your bones: *You do not have to earn your right to rest. You do not have to be productive to be worthy of love or belonging. You are enough as you are, even when you're still.*

## Meet Alisa

Alisa came to mentoring overwhelmed and emotionally drained. A 42-year-old gifted professional and creative, she described her life as a constant chase: "I wake up already behind. Even on weekends, I can't relax without guilt. There's always more to do, more to prove." Despite years of success, awards, leadership roles, a respected reputation, she confessed that she never felt like she was doing *enough*.

Underneath her polished exterior was a lifetime of internalized pressure. Labeled "advanced" in school, Alisa had been praised for her achievements but rarely supported in her sensitivities or energy patterns. As a neurodivergent adult, she now experienced cycles of hyperfocus followed by debilitating fatigue, which she interpreted as personal failure. She pushed through exhaustion, only to crash—then blamed herself for the crash.

In our work together, we began gently peeling back the beliefs that had shaped her inner world. She recognized that her identity had been entangled with productivity: if she wasn't achieving, she feared she would be forgotten, dismissed, or seen as lazy.

Through reflective exercises, values clarification, and nervous system care, Alisa began to shift. She started honoring her body's need for spaciousness. She created an "unstructured hour" each day where she was not allowed to *achieve*, only to rest, notice, or play. At first, it felt unbearable. But over time, it became sacred.

Alisa redefined success: not as getting everything done, but as staying connected to herself while doing what mattered most. She began writing again, not for clients or deadlines, but for joy. She noticed that when she moved from alignment instead of fear, her work became more impactful and far less draining.

One day, she said, "I'm no longer measuring my life by output. I'm measuring it by *presence*." That was the moment she reclaimed her worth.

As we unravel the pressure to constantly produce, we create space for something deeper to emerge: a more intuitive, embodied way of moving through the world. This shift naturally invites us into the next vital practice *the art of slowing down.* When we slow down, we don't lose momentum, we gain clarity, presence, and connection to the pulse of our own life. Let's explore what it means to honor that slower, wiser rhythm next.

## Reflection Questions

1. What messages did you receive growing up about productivity and success? How have they shaped your sense of worth?

2. When do you feel most disconnected from yourself in the pursuit of "getting things done"?

3. How does your natural energy cycle function? Are there times of day, week, or month when you feel most creative or alive?

4. What forms of rest, creativity, or connection have you devalued because they didn't appear "productive"?

5. If productivity were defined by alignment instead of output, what would change in your daily life?

CHAPTER 30

# NAVIGATING SPECIAL INTERESTS AND HYPERFOCUS

For many neurodivergent individuals, especially those with ADHD and autism, special interests and hyperfocus are not quirks; they are central to how we process the world, access joy, and express our gifts. Yet these deeply immersive experiences are often misunderstood by others, pathologized by systems, or even turned against us internally when they don't fit the "productivity" narrative.

Special interests are not distractions. They are *portals*. They provide direction, comfort, clarity, and sometimes even healing. They are how many of us regulate, engage, and explore life in technicolor. Hyperfocus, too, is often seen as a problem when it becomes intense or all-consuming. But when channeled consciously, it can become a superpower, a deep well of presence that gives birth to brilliance.

The key is not to suppress these parts of ourselves, but to learn how to navigate them honoring their power while developing awareness of how they affect our energy, relationships, and wellbeing.

**The Language of the Soul**
In my mentoring work with gifted and neurodivergent adults, I've seen that special interests are often more than hobbies. They are soul languages, expressions of a deep inner truth. They give us

access to ourselves when words fall short. They create a bridge between inner and outer worlds.

For some, a special interest is a lifelong passion. For others, it changes like seasons, cycling through topics or themes with intensity and awe. And while the outside world may see it as "obsession," it is often where we feel most alive, connected, and whole.

The same is true of hyperfocus. When you're in it, time distorts. Hunger disappears. The world fades away. You are *one* with what you're doing. This state can be deeply nourishing when entered voluntarily and excited with care. But when we lose track of time, needs, or boundaries, hyperfocus can lead to depletion and disorientation. Awareness is key.

Learning to navigate these experiences means honoring them as part of your sacred design, while also building rituals to help you ground, pause, and return to balance.

**Navigating With Awareness**

To live well with special interests and hyperfocus, we must move from *reaction* to *relationship*. This means:
- **Honoring the sacredness of your passions** instead of trying to dilute or justify them.
- **Creating gentle entry and exit rituals** so your nervous system doesn't get stuck in the extremes of all-or-nothing.
- **Educating those close to you** so they understand your cycles and needs without judgment
- **Letting go of shame** around how you spend your time, especially when it doesn't look "balanced" to the outside world.

Your interests are not random. They're revealing something about who you are, what you value, and how you were designed to experience life. The goal is not to be less intense, it's to become more intentional.

**The Dual Nature of Hyperfocus**

Hyperfocus is one of the most powerful and most challenging

experiences for many neurodivergent individuals. It's the state of full cognitive and emotional immersion, where time dissolves and nothing else exists but the object of your attention. In hyperfocus, we may create brilliant work, solve complex problems, or enter states of flow that feel transcendent.

But hyperfocus can also lead to neglect of basic needs food, sleep, movement, connection. It can become a form of escape when life feels unmanageable. And it can be disorienting when it ends, leaving behind a crash of fatigue or a sense of emptiness.

As with many neurodivergent traits, hyperfocus is not good or bad, it's a tool. And like any powerful tool, it requires mindful stewardship.

## Special Interests as Soul Anchors

In my mentoring work, I often describe special interests as "soul anchors" threads of meaning that help neurodivergent individuals remain tethered to themselves in a chaotic or overwhelming world. These interests are not just hobbies. They are portals into wonder, mastery, and identity.

When we allow ourselves to follow what lights us up, we open space for joy, self-trust, and nervous system regulation. The challenge is not in having special interests, it's in giving ourselves permission to value them, even when others don't understand them.

Rather than asking how to "control" these interests, you can ask:
- How does this interest support my emotional or cognitive regulation?
- When does it nourish me, and when does it deplete me?
- How can I structure my time or space to honor this interest without sacrificing balance?

## Meet Bradley

Bradley is a 36-year-old Autistic and ADHD adult who came to mentoring, experiencing both feelings of empowerment and frustration by his tendency to hyperfocus. "When I'm in the zone, I can create amazing things," he said. "But I forget to eat, ignore texts, and then crash hard. It feels like a gift and a trap."

Bradley's current passion is urban architecture. He had spent weeks researching obscure zoning laws and drafting city redesigns on top of his full-time job. His partner expressed concern, noting that he often seemed unreachable during these periods.

Through our sessions, Bradley began to see his special interests not as something to "control," but as something to *steward*. He learned to build soft boundaries around his hyperfocus sessions: setting a timer with a gentle chime, placing snacks and water within reach, and scheduling "re-entry time" after a deep dive.

We also worked on de-shaming the idea of needing recovery time after intense focus. Bradley realized that the crash wasn't failure, it was simply his body asking for integration.

Eventually, he began sharing his insights and designs with a local community board, turning his passion into service. What once felt like an isolating spiral became a cycle of creation, reflection, and contribution.

Bradley's story is a beautiful example of what happens when we stop trying to "fix" our intensity and instead learn to flow with it.

## Reflection Questions

1. What have your special interests taught you about yourself and how have they helped you feel more alive or grounded?

2. How do you currently experience hyperfocus? What are the benefits and costs for you personally?

3. What boundaries or rituals could you create to help you enter and exit deep focus with more care and less depletion?

4. Are there any old messages of shame or judgment around your passions that you're ready to release?

5. How might you reframe your special interests as spiritual or soul-centered practices rather than distractions?

# CHAPTER 31

# HOW TO CHASE BIG DREAMS WITHOUT MELTING DOWN

Big dreams live in the DNA of the neurodivergent soul. Whether you're a visionary, an intuitive, a gifted creator, or a sensitive guide your inner landscape is alive with possibility. You see connections others miss. You feel the pull of what *could be* as vivid as what already is. This kind of dreaming is not naive, it's essential. It is how progress, beauty, and breakthroughs come into the world.

But chasing big dreams comes with a cost, especially for the neurodivergent. Our nervous systems are often more reactive. Our minds race ahead while our bodies beg for rest. Our emotional depth means we feel the wins and losses more acutely. And when external structures don't accommodate our pacing, processing, or perception, the result can be burnout, shutdown, or emotional overwhelm. In short, the very dreams that fuel us can also fry us.

As I often tell my clients: *"Your big dreams are real and valid, but your nervous system must be on the journey with you, not dragging behind in panic."* We must learn to dream big *and* regulate deeply. We must grow our capacity to expand without collapsing. That is the heart of sustainable soul work.

## The Double Bind of the Gifted Dreamer

Many neurodivergent individuals experience what I call the *gifted double bind*: an internal conflict between the magnitude of your vision and the limitations of your current energy, environment, or support systems. You may feel like you're "too much" for the people around you, and "not enough" to actually do what you see is possible. This paradox can lead to paralysis, shame, and eventual withdrawal.

The truth is, dreaming and doing operate on different frequencies. Your dream self is expansive, intuitive, and visionary. Your "doing" self is practical, embodied, and grounded in real-time. Most meltdowns happen when we skip the integration between these two parts. We push through, override signals, and expect ourselves to perform at visionary levels without tending to our basic needs.

As I wrote in *The Loneliness Cure*: "Burnout often masquerades as failure, when in reality it is the soul's cry for rhythm, rest, and reconnection." Big dreams require equally big care structures, emotional, physical, spiritual, and relational.

## Meet Travis

Travis is a 33-year-old autistic and gifted entrepreneur who had a powerful vision to revolutionize how neurodivergent students access mentorship. His idea was strong, his purpose clear, and his passion undeniable. He launched with energy and excitement, working long days and networking late into the night. Within six months, he landed investors, signed several schools onto a pilot program, and was featured in a major online publication.

But behind the scenes, Travis was unraveling. He stopped sleeping well. His sensory sensitivities were flaring. He was snapping at his team and questioning his own competence. "I've never wanted something more," he told me, "but I feel like I'm breaking under the weight of it."

When we worked together, we uncovered a familiar cycle: Travis was chasing his dream at the cost of his regulation. He was trying to prove his worth through output and speed, unknowingly recreating the same perfectionist trauma patterns from his childhood where only achievement earned love and safety.

With support, Travis began implementing daily nervous system check-ins. He restructured his week to include "quiet buffer days" after high-stimulation events. He built a small inner circle of trusted advisors who could help him slow down without losing momentum.

Over time, Travis realized that chasing his dream didn't mean sprinting, it meant staying emotionally resourced for the long game. "When I stopped trying to win the race and started tending to the ground I was running on," he said, "the path became a lot more sustainable and a lot more joyful."

## Anchoring Practices for Sustainable Dream-Chasing

Here are some guiding practices I teach my clients when they're pursuing bold visions:

- **Work with your cycles, not against them.** Your energy is not linear. Dreamers need downtime. Build intentional pauses into your pursuit.
- **Create emotional scaffolding.** Who holds space for your doubts, fears, and overthinking? Build a support team that includes both strategy and soul care.
- **Set soul-aligned metrics.** Instead of "how fast?" ask "how true?" How does this next step align with your values and energy?
- **Regulate before you reach.** Tend to your nervous system first. Don't pitch, launch, or decide when you're dysregulated.
- **Honor grief and celebration equally.** Every new expansion asks you to let go of something. Make space to feel both the stretch and the shedding.

As I often say: "Your dream is sacred but so is your breath. Chase your calling with your nervous system in tow." Your dreams are not the problem, your nervous system is simply asking to be part of the plan. By learning to pace yourself, listen to your inner rhythms, and stay rooted in self-trust, you give your big vision a steady foundation.

## Reflection Questions

1. What big dream or vision currently lives in your heart? How do you relate to it? Does it feel inspiring, overwhelming, or both?

2. When you imagine taking action toward that dream, what sensations show up in your body?

3. Are there parts of your dream that feel urgent, even panicky? Where might that urgency come from trauma, conditioning, comparison?

4. What rhythms does your body prefer when creating or working toward something meaningful?

5. Who can support you in holding your vision without pushing you past your limits?

6. What boundaries would protect your energy while keeping your dream alive?

## CHAPTER 32

# SUCCESS DYSPHORIA: WHEN ACHIEVEMENT FEELS EMPTY

It's a strange and painful thing to accomplish what you set out to do and feel nothing. Or worse, to feel guilt, disconnection, or despair in the very place where you expected fulfillment. For many gifted and neurodivergent individuals, this experience has a name: success dysphoria, a dissonance between outer achievement and inner reality.

Success dysphoria arises when the goals you worked so hard to reach do not match your internal values, energy, or sense of self. You may receive praise, promotions, or recognition, but instead of joy, you feel numb, anxious, or like an imposter. You wonder: Is this all there is? And sometimes more hauntingly: If even this doesn't fulfill me, what will?

This isn't because you're ungrateful. It's because you were never taught to define success on your own terms. Instead, you were conditioned to chase what looked impressive, acceptable, or secure. And in doing so, you may have wandered far from your true inner compass.

**The Root of the Disconnect**
Success dysphoria is often the result of living by someone else's script. You may have been praised early on for being smart, capable, or "going places." From there, a quiet pressure built to always exceed, to stand out, to rise above. But many gifted and neurodivergent people

mask their difficulties so well that others only see their capabilities, not the cost.

So, you pushed. You achieved. You climbed. And then you got there, and didn't feel like yourself anymore.

In my mentoring work, I often meet brilliant adults who have checked all the boxes, degrees, careers, accolades, only to discover they feel more lost than ever. Their soul isn't in what they've built. Their bodies are tired. Their creativity is dormant. They no longer know who they are when they're not performing.

Success without authenticity creates spiritual dissonance. And that dissonance, if not addressed, turns into burnout, isolation, or a perpetual sense of not being enough, no matter how much you accomplish.

## Healing Through Redefinition

To move through success dysphoria, we must first name it as real not as entitlement, weakness, or failure, but as *data* from the soul. Your discomfort is telling you something vital: you're ready to return to a life that reflects *you*, not just your résumé.

The healing begins with redefinition.

- What if success looked like waking up with ease instead of dread?
- What if it meant having time to create, rest, or be fully present with loved ones?
- What if it was less about visibility and more about *alignment*?

When you allow your nervous system and inner wisdom to lead, success begins to feel different. It softens. It deepens. It may not look flashy on the outside, but it feels nourishing from within.

Success doesn't have to be sacrificed; it has to be *realigned*. In your rhythm. In your voice. In your truth.

## The Subtle Forms of Success

For the neurodivergent soul, success often shows up in unconventional ways:

- Regulating your nervous system after years of survival mode
- Saying no to something that drains you, even if others approve of it
- Reclaiming your creative joy without needing to monetize it
- Creating a life that honors your sensory needs and emotional cycles
- Feeling at home in your own body, finally

These forms of success are not always seen or celebrated by society yet they are soul milestones. They mark the turning point from survival to embodiment.

**Integration and Embodiment**
Moving forward after success dysphoria doesn't mean abandoning everything you've built. It means asking: "What parts of this still reflect me? What needs to be released or reshaped? What does my soul want to build now, in its own voice and time? This process is not about perfection. It's about reclamation.

You are allowed to outgrow old dreams. You are allowed to pause without a plan. You are allowed to begin again with tenderness. The next version of your life doesn't have to be bigger. It has to be truer.

**Reflection Questions**

1. When have you felt the most disconnected from your achievements and what did you notice in your body and emotions at that time?

2. Whose definition of success have you been living by? Whose approval have you been chasing, consciously or unconsciously?

3. What parts of your current life or work feel authentic and what feels performative or misaligned?

4. What would success look and feel like if it were rooted in your nervous system's rhythm and your soul's truth?

5. What is one small act you can take this week to honor your *own* definition of success, even quietly?

# CHAPTER 33

# SUSTAINABLE PURPOSE: YOUR RIGHT TO A GENTLE LIFE

So many gifted and neurodivergent souls carry a deep longing to make a difference, to live with purpose, contribute meaningfully, and align their work with their values. We feel the suffering of the world acutely, sense the gaps between what is and what could be, and often feel called to bridge them. Here is what is often missed: you don't have to sacrifice your well-being to live your purpose. Purpose is meant to *sustain* you. It is not meant to burn you out.

We live in a culture that equates purpose with hustle and urgency. The message is loud and clear: if you really care, you'll push harder. But the neurodivergent system often doesn't thrive in that paradigm. We are sensitive, perceptive, and deep-feeling—and that means we require gentleness not as a luxury, but as a necessity. You have a right to a life that nourishes you, not just one that demands from you.

**Redefining Purpose on Your Terms**
Purpose doesn't have to be grandiose. It doesn't have to come with a title, a platform, or a measurable output. Your purpose might show up in small, sacred acts: the way you listen to someone without rushing them, the way you create beauty out of chaos, the way you hold space for truth in a world addicted to noise.

In my mentoring practice, I often guide clients through the process of untangling their identity from external expectations. Many arrive with an inherited script, *"Make something of yourself,"* or *"Don't waste your potential."* These scripts are often tied to perfectionism, people-pleasing, or the chronic fear of not doing enough.

But when you slow down and listen to your own rhythms, a different form of purpose emerges, one that is both *sustainable* and deeply authentic. It may be quieter. It may not impress everyone. But it will fit *you*.

## Gentle Doesn't Mean Living Small

Let's be clear: living a gentle life doesn't mean living a small life. It means choosing alignment over approval. It means recognizing that your value is not in how much you give, but in how true you are to yourself as you give.

Gentleness allows for depth. It honors your cycles. It lets your nervous system soften and your soul breathe.

You don't need to earn the right to rest. You don't need to carry the world to justify your existence. Your presence is purposeful. And that purpose is allowed to unfold in sustainable, life-affirming ways.

## Meet Anna

Anna was a 47-year-old neurodivergent artist and consultant who came to mentoring after a major health crisis. "I feel like my body had to scream to get me to stop," she said during our first session. A lifetime of over-functioning, taking on too much, saying yes when she meant no, constantly trying to be everything to everyone, had led to total exhaustion.

Anna had always believed her purpose was to "help others rise." But helping, for her, had become self-abandonment. She spent so much energy anticipating the needs of others that she couldn't hear her own.

In our work together, Anna began the radical process of slowing down. She reclaimed mornings for herself. She stopped filling every moment with doing. She allowed her art to be expressive rather than productive. At first, this felt like failure. But slowly, a new sense of self emerged softer, but truer.

Eventually, Anna redefined her purpose as *being a gentle witness to beauty and change.* She still worked with others, only now from a spacious place with healthy, functional boundaries. Her energy became more focused, her body more regulated, her soul more at peace. "I used to think I had to prove I mattered," she told me. "Now I know that living gently *is* the proof."

## Reflection Questions

1. What messages have you internalized about purpose, productivity, or self-worth that may no longer serve you?

2. What does a *gentle life* look and feel like to you? Are there ways you're already living it without giving yourself credit?

3. Where are you over-functioning in the name of purpose or service—and what might it look like to step back or soften?

4. What small actions bring you a sense of quiet fulfillment, even if no one else sees or praises them?

5. How can you begin aligning your purpose with your energy, sensitivity, and authentic pace instead of societal expectations?

## PART 6

# SOUL CARE AS A LIFELONG PRACTICE

CHAPTER 34

# CYCLES OF ENERGY AND SHUTDOWN

You have inner rhythms. Living with a neurodivergent nervous system often means inhabiting a body that doesn't move through time or effort in a linear way. Energy flows in waves, not straight lines. This truth is one of the most misunderstood and often pathologized aspects of neurodivergent life. While the world around us is built on productivity models that reward consistency, predictability, and stamina, the internal landscape of many neurodivergent individuals moves according to very different laws, ones that resemble nature more than machines.

There are days when the mind feels lit from within, ideas arrive in floods, connections spark like fire, and the body is buoyed by a mysterious, almost otherworldly energy. During these periods, work may feel effortless, conversations animated, and intuition razor-sharp. These times can feel like being plugged into a divine current, alive with possibility and purpose. But just as naturally, just as inevitably, that current withdraws. The system falters. Fatigue settles in like fog, sometimes suddenly, other times gradually, and the brightness dims.

For many neurodivergent people, this ebb in energy is not a sign of laziness, disinterest, or inconsistency, it is the body's intelligence calling for restoration. Shutdowns, fatigue, and withdrawal are not failures; they are part of a sacred rhythm. They are protective mechanisms of a finely tuned system that often runs hot in a world that offers little space for rest. Just as the tides rise and fall, so too does the energy of the neurodivergent soul.

What is often labeled as "burnout" is sometimes simply the culmination of accumulated misattunement, overriding sensory needs, forcing social engagement, or meeting expectations that were never designed with your neurotype in mind. Over time, this suppression of self-expressed rhythms becomes internalized. Many neurodivergent adults carry a deep shame about their energy patterns, having been told their whole lives that their pace is "too much," "too slow," "too inconsistent," or "too unpredictable."

But within these cycles lies profound wisdom. They teach us that energy is not a commodity to be squeezed from the soul; it is a living, breathing force that moves in cycles of creation and integration, action and rest, light and shadow. Honoring these cycles is not indulgent. It is a revolutionary act of self-respect. It is the foundation of sustainable soul care.

When we stop judging ourselves through the lens of productivity and begin to attune to our natural rhythms, we create space for something transformative: trust. Trust in the body's messages. Trust in the soul's timing. Trust that rest is not the absence of progress but an integral part of it. In this way, caring for the neurodivergent soul becomes less about fixing ourselves to meet the world, and more about building lives and practices that meet us where we are.

This is not an easy task in a world that often demands uniformity and hustle. But it is a necessary one. And over time, it can become a form of liberation.

## Honoring Your Cycles

Caring for your neurodivergent soul means developing a relationship with your energy flow. This is about listening and pausing long enough to notice when your body whispers instead of waiting for it to shout. It requires self-trust, especially when the world does not mirror your internal rhythm.

Soul care becomes a lifelong practice when you stop demanding consistency from yourself and start embracing coherence and attunement to what is real and alive inside you at any given moment. Honoring your personal cycle of energy is a vital aspect for your soul care.

Your cycles may not align with the external expectations of those around you or the culture at large. Remember that they carry their own inner intelligence and it may or may not resonate with you from time to time. Recognizing and respecting your personal rhythms and energy cycles is a radical act of self-compassion.

## Meet Meghan

Meghan is a gifted, autistic adult in her early 40s, working as a freelance graphic designer. Her inner world is vibrant colors, patterns, and sensory impressions dance vividly in her mind. She can hyperfocus for hours when a project inspires her, producing breathtaking designs that feel like soul expressions.

But this comes at a cost. After a week of creative output, Meghan often crashes. Her body aches. Words become difficult. She becomes irritable and hypersensitive to sound. The world feels too loud, and she retreats into silence for days. Early in her career, Meghan internalized this as failure. She believed she was unreliable, too sensitive, not "professional enough."

In therapy, Meghan began mapping her energy. She noticed a rhythm, a personal cycle that moved through inspiration, intensity, burnout, and recovery. Her shutdowns weren't regressions; they were messages from her nervous system asking for care and re-regulation. She began planning her projects with built-in rest periods and learned to communicate her energy rhythms to clients who valued her brilliance.

Over time, Meghan stopped fighting her shutdowns. Instead, she welcomed them as part of her neurodivergent ecology. She learned to nourish herself during low-energy times through quiet rituals: sensory deprivation, journaling, herbal tea, weighted blankets. What once felt like collapse now felt like restoration.

## Reflection Questions

1. What are the distinct phases of your energy cycle? How do you typically feel, act, or think in each?

2. How have you interpreted shutdowns or low-energy periods in the past? What stories have you told yourself about them?

3. What sensory or emotional signals indicate you are nearing shutdown? How could you respond differently in those moments?

4. What supportive rituals or boundaries could you implement to honor your energy rhythms?

5. Who in your life respects your natural cycles? How could you deepen those connections or advocate for more understanding where needed?

## CHAPTER 35

# SOUL ANCHORS – PRACTICES THAT REGULATE AND RENEW

To be neurodivergent in a neurotypical world often means living in a state of chronic adaptation constantly interpreting, translating, filtering, and managing internal experiences that do not fit the external environment. Over time, this can lead to profound energetic depletion and disconnection from the self. In the swirl of overstimulation, sensory fragmentation, and emotional intensity, it becomes essential to find *anchors, practices*, rituals, and relationships that return us to ourselves. It is vital to find grounding in a world that pulls you away from your center.

A soul anchor is not a tool for fixing or normalizing; it is a living practice that gently restores coherence between the inner world and the outer one. Anchors remind us that we are allowed to come home to ourselves again and again, especially when the world becomes too much.

These practices are not prescriptive. What anchors a neurodivergent person may overwhelm another. For one, it might be a silent time in nature, walking barefoot in the grass or watching the movement of trees. For another, it might be engaging in structured movement, listening to the same song on repeat, or immersing in a favorite sensory texture like a soft blanket or warm water. The anchor is defined not by form, but by its effect: it brings the soul back into presence.

Anchoring is not about control, regulation for the sake of performance, or enforcing "calm." Many neurodivergent people have been told to regulate only in service of becoming less disruptive, more productive, or easier to manage. But true regulation, as a soul practice, is about reconnection. It is about reweaving the threads between body, mind, and spirit after they've been frayed by sensory overload, emotional chaos, or social exhaustion.

When we begin to consciously seek out and commit to soul-anchoring practices, we are declaring that our internal experiences matter. We are resisting the pressure to keep pushing through and instead saying: "I am worth the pause. I am worth the care. I deserve to be well in my own way".

## The Sacred Simplicity of Return

In a culture obsessed with optimization, soul care through anchoring practices can feel almost radical in its simplicity. We are not talking about grand transformations or complicated wellness plans. We are talking about accessible, repeatable, intuitive acts that remind your system that it is safe, that it belongs, and that it is worthy of care.

Anchors help us mark the moments between energy and shutdown, between presence and dissociation. They are the small sacred gestures that keep us tethered to ourselves when the world wants to pull us away. Over time, they become a language of self-trust.

For the neurodivergent soul, the practice of returning again and again is devotion to your highest good.

## Meet Christopher

Christopher is a twice-exceptional man in his early 30s, a gifted writer with ADHD and sensory processing sensitivity. His thoughts come fast and bright, sometimes too fast for his body to keep up. He often forgets to eat, skips sleep during hyperfocus spells, and finds himself emotionally flooded after social gatherings, even ones he enjoys.

For most of his life, Christopher believed that self-regulation meant suppression, biting his tongue, holding in stimming, pretending not to be overwhelmed by noise. But this strategy led to regular shutdowns and cycles of burnout.

It wasn't until he began working with a somatic coach who understood neurodivergence that Christopher reframed his relationship to regulation. Together, they created what he calls *anchor rituals*, not strict routines, but living, adaptable practices he can return to when he feels scattered or overstimulated.

Christopher's anchors include:
- Lighting a candle at his desk before writing to signal a transition into focused time.
- Laying on the floor with noise-canceling headphones and a weighted blanket after social interactions.
- Reciting a short affirmation out loud: "I am allowed to come back to my body."
- Using scent as an anchor, carrying a small essential oil roller that reminds him of his grandmother's garden, a place of deep safety.

These practices are not dramatic. They don't "solve" his sensory or attentional differences. But they help him return. When the world spins fast, Christopher now has a way to say, "Here I am. I'm not lost. I can hold myself through this".

## Reflection Questions

1. What activities, environments, or sensory experiences help you feel the most present in your body? Can you name 2–3 that feel restorative rather than draining?

2. When you feel overstimulated or emotionally flooded, what do you currently do to find your way back? Is that response helpful or inherited from past survival strategies?

3. Are there moments in your daily life where an anchoring ritual might offer a gentle transition (e.g., before bed, after work, after overstimulating social time)?

4. What kinds of regulation have you been taught are "acceptable" or "unacceptable"? How has that shaped the way you treat your own needs?

5. Imagine a version of your daily life where soul-anchoring practices are seen as essential, not optional. What would need to shift to make space for that vision?

# CHAPTER 36

# REDEFINING RESILIENCE – HEALING ON YOUR OWN TERMS

There is a myth of the Bounced-Back Life that refers to the perceived resilience you have in stressful times. Often, the price you pay is greater than you or others may account for day to day. Resilience is often defined by how quickly and efficiently someone "bounces back" after adversity, how fast they return to work, rejoin the social world, or put on a brave face. This definition is rooted in performance and productivity, not in healing. For the neurodivergent soul, deep feeling, differently wired, and often chronically overstimulated, this version of resilience can feel more like erasure than empowerment.

In truth, resilience for the neurodivergent does not always look like getting back up quickly. Sometimes it looks like lying down longer. It looks like grieving fully before rebuilding, like unraveling patterns that were never ours to begin with. It looks like daring to heal in slow, circular, nonlinear ways that make room for shutdowns, regressions, and soul-deep rest.

We must reclaim the definition of resilience from systems that value endurance over integration. For the neurodivergent person, true resilience is not about how much one can endure, but how honestly one can listen to the body's limits, how gently one can tend to the nervous system, and how courageously one can live in alignment with inner truth.

Resilience on your own terms is a radical redefinition. It is saying: *"I will not use recovery as a race. I will not use healing as a way to earn my worth. I will heal as I am, in the language and rhythm of my own soul."*

## What Healing Really Asks of Us

Redefining resilience means to reject the performance of strength and instead root yourself in the practice of authentic presence. It means letting go of shame when the body needs more rest, more time, more space. It means honoring the inner child who learned to survive by suppressing needs and now longs to be heard.

Healing, when done soulfully, does not erase our neurodivergence. It doesn't aim to make us more like the world around us. Instead, it teaches us to live more fully inside our truth, to integrate the tender parts, and to become safe havens for ourselves.

There is no finish line. No medal for the fastest recovery. What matters is that we are healing on our own terms with compassion, curiosity, and the audacity to slow down in a world that idolizes speed.

Resilience, then, becomes less about rising quickly and more about returning wholly. To the body. To the truth. To the soul.

## Meet Kiara

Kiara is a late identified twice exceptional (2e) woman in her mid-50s who spent most of her life masking. As a child, she was praised for her maturity and intelligence but secretly suffered from sensory overload, deep anxiety, and emotional confusion. She spent decades pushing herself into a high-pressure corporate job, into over-scheduled social commitments, into roles she thought she *should* play. She learned to survive by overachieving and numbing out.

When her nervous system finally collapsed in her early 40s, she called it a breakdown. Doctors called it burnout. But Kiara knew something more profound was happening, something spiritual. Her old life no longer fits. Her body was speaking truths she could no longer ignore.

In the years that followed, Kiara began what she calls her "spiral path" of healing. It wasn't linear. She had moments of great insight and peace, followed by periods of deep exhaustion and grief. Sometimes she felt like she was regressing. Other times, she felt reborn. Through it all, she chose to trust the deeper rhythm, even when the world urged her to "move on."

Today, Kiara lives a slower, quieter life. She spends time in her garden, writes poetry, and connects with other neurodivergent women who are also reclaiming their truth. She still experiences shutdowns. She still has days when masking creeps in. She no longer sees these moments as setbacks. She sees them as part of the spiral, reminders that healing isn't about perfection, but presence.

## Reflection Questions

1. What messages about resilience did you receive growing up? How have those shaped your expectations of yourself?

2. When you experience setbacks, shutdowns, or overwhelm, how do you typically respond? What stories do you tell yourself about what that means?

3. What might resilience look like if it centered your actual needs, instead of societal expectations?

4. In what ways have you already shown resilience, quiet, unseen, or soul-deep that deserves to be honored?

5. What would healing on your own terms feel like? What would you need to give yourself permission to release or embrace?

CHAPTER 37

# SPIRITUALITY BEYOND DOGMA - RECLAIMING THE SACRED ON YOUR OWN TERMS

Your soul is longing for something more. That something more is your heart's desire. Sadly, you may be shying away from your heart's desire for fear of not being able to attain it or because you cannot yet see how you will reach the goals.

For many neurodivergent souls, the pull toward the sacred is not abstract, it is embodied, intuitive, and deeply felt. We often live with a heightened sensitivity to unseen currents, a porousness to emotional and energetic fields, and a persistent sense that there is *more* to this life than what meets the eye. Whether we have language for it or not, many of us carry an inner knowing that whispers of connection, mystery, and divine intelligence.

And yet, the road to spiritual belonging is often fraught. Traditional religious systems, particularly those steeped in rigid dogma, hierarchy, or punitive frameworks have not always welcomed the neurodivergent. We are the ones who ask too many questions, feel too deeply, and sense what others ignore. We may have been told our instincts were wrong, our bodies sinful, our insights heretical, or our visions delusional. In response, many of us learned to hide our spiritual sensitivities, or to sever them entirely.

This disconnection leaves a particular ache in the neurodivergent soul, a longing not only to reconnect with something greater than the self, but to do so in a way that doesn't require betrayal of the self. What we seek is not a set of rules to follow, but a way of being in the world that feels *true, alive,* and *inclusive of our whole selves.*

Spirituality beyond dogma is not a rejection of the sacred; it is a return to it. It is a reclaiming of the right to have direct, personal, embodied, and intuitive experiences of the divine, whatever name we give it. It is the freedom to craft a relationship with mystery that honors neurodivergent perception, emotional depth, and the soul's inner compass.

For some, this might mean reconnecting with a spiritual tradition through a lens of healing. For others, it might mean forging an entirely new path, one guided by nature, dreams, art, ancestors, or inner knowing. There is no one right way. What matters is that the path allows you to be fully present as *you*, not as someone edited to fit a mold.

To walk a spiritual path as a neurodivergent person is to honor the sacredness of difference. It is to believe that your sensitivities, your visions, your deep questions, and your desire for transcendence are not liabilities to be tamed, but gifts to be cultivated. It is to claim that your way of connecting with the sacred is valid even if it doesn't look like anyone else's.

In this space, we invite a spirituality that liberates rather than confines, that nourishes rather than shames. A spirituality that allows you to *belong to yourself* while belonging to something greater. This is not an easy journey, but it is a holy one.

## Spiritual Pathways that Welcome the Neurodivergent Soul

Not all spiritual roads require conformity. In fact, many traditions, especially earth-based, mystical, or contemplative ones have long embraced those who see and feel differently. Neurodivergent individuals often find resonance in spiritual expressions that mirror their inner world: nonlinear, symbolic, sensory-rich, and relational. Below are a few paths and practices that many neurodivergent people find regulating, meaningful, and expansive.

## 1. Nature-Based and Earth-Honoring Spirituality

Many neurodivergent souls feel most at ease in the natural world. The quiet order of trees, the rhythm of waves, the presence of animals all offer companionship without demand. Nature-based spirituality invites the whole body into the experience. It honors cycles, diversity, and connection beyond words.

For some, this may look like walking meditation, observing moon phases, growing a garden, or practicing animism, the belief that all things carry spirit and consciousness. It's a space where sensory perception is not only welcomed, but sacred.

## 2. Intuitive and Mystical Practices

The neurodivergent mind often excels in symbolic thinking, abstract connection, and nonlinear perception making intuitive practices feel like home. Divination tools (like tarot, oracle cards, or runes), dream work, and energy healing can offer non-verbal pathways to self-understanding and divine communion.

These practices don't demand dogma. They invite dialogue with the unknown. And for many, they provide a mirror to one's inner truth without judgment or hierarchy.

## 3. Creative and Artistic Expression as Devotion

For those who struggle with spoken prayer or formal rituals, creativity itself can become a sacred act. Painting, singing, dancing, writing are not just hobbies, but the ways the soul speaks. Artistic ritual allows for expression that bypasses the need for explanation. The canvas, the voice, the clay all becomes portals to the sacred.

Neurodivergent people often report feeling most connected to something greater than themselves when they're in creative flow. In that state, the world softens, and the soul stretches out in joy.

### 4. Ancestral and Cultural Reclamation

Some neurodivergent people find spiritual grounding in reconnecting with ancestral practices especially if those practices were colonized, erased, or stigmatized. This path may include learning traditional songs, foods, ceremonies, or cosmologies from one's lineage.

The process of ancestral healing is especially resonant for those who've lived with identity fragmentation. It offers a rootedness that says: *You come from people who prayed, created, survived. You are not alone in your sensitivity.*

### 5. Sensory and Somatic Rituals

Because neurodivergent bodies often process information differently, embodied spirituality can be deeply anchoring. Lighting a specific candle, rocking while reciting a prayer, wearing a familiar texture during meditation, these small, sensory-aligned acts bring the divine *into* the body rather than keeping it at a distance.

For many, sacredness is felt not in belief, but in sensation. It's the way the light filters through the trees. The vibration of a chant. The scent of something beloved. These are not lesser forms of spirituality. They are gateways.

### A Coming Home That Does Not Require Disappearing

Perhaps the most revolutionary act a neurodivergent soul can take is to build a spiritual life that requires no masking. One where you don't have to edit your questions, mute your senses, or shrink your truth. A path where the Divine is not a distant authority figure, but a presence that welcomes all of you, especially the parts you were told to hide.

Spirituality beyond dogma says: *You are already whole. You don't need to be fixed to be holy.* You are free to shape your own relationship with the sacred. Free to create rituals that work for your nervous system. Free to listen to the voice within, even if it doesn't sound like the voice of your former teachers. Free to follow wonder instead of fear. This freedom isn't chaos. It is reverence. Reverence for your own neurotype, for your lived experience, and for the ways your soul is uniquely wired to perceive the sacred.

## Meet Marisol

Marisol is a multiple neurodivergent woman in her early 40s who grew up in a deeply religious environment. Raised in a strict, authoritarian household that demanded obedience and punished deviation, she quickly learned that questioning was dangerous. She was bright, emotionally intense, and spiritually curious qualities that were often pathologized as rebellion or pride. By adolescence, she had internalized a deep shame around her sensitivity and intuition.

After leaving home, Marisol swung between spiritual starvation and spiritual seeking. She tried on various belief systems, but each time, the structure began to feel tight around her soul. Rules, hierarchies, and the need to conform would trigger shutdowns and anxiety. Something in her body would say, "This isn't safe. This isn't home".

It wasn't until her autism diagnosis in her late 30s that she began to see her patterns in a new light. She realized that her spiritual sensitivity wasn't a flaw, it was part of her neurotype. Her resistance to dogma wasn't defiance, it was protection. She stopped trying to make herself fit into spiritual containers that weren't built for her and instead began building her own altar both literally and metaphorically.

Marisol's current spiritual practice includes:
- Daily nature walks where she listens to birdsong like prayer.
- An altar in her bedroom with objects that carry ancestral meaning: stones, feathers, family photos, handwritten prayers.
- Dream journaling and lunar rituals that help her honor the nonlinear rhythms of her body and mind.
- A personal mantra: *"I don't need to earn sacredness. I am sacred because I exist."*

Her spirituality is fluid, intuitive, and deeply relational. It doesn't need a label. It simply needs her presence. And that, she's learned, is more than enough.

**Reflection Questions**

1. What early messages did you receive about spirituality or God? How did they shape your self-image as a neurodivergent person?

2. Are there spiritual practices or beliefs you've held onto out of fear or habit, but that no longer feel alive or true to you?

3. When and where do you most easily feel a connection to something greater than yourself?

4. What would a spiritual practice designed around your actual needs, sensory, emotional, energetic look and feel like?

5. How might you begin reclaiming your own sacred path, even in small, sensory, or intuitive ways?

## CHAPTER 38

# REBUILDING TRUST WITH YOUR NERVOUS SYSTEM

Learning to live in the body without bracing is very important to your long-term health and life satisfaction. For many neurodivergent souls, the body has never felt like a safe place to live. From a young age, we may have experienced our bodies as "too much" or "not enough." Too loud. Too sensitive. Too reactive. We may have been punished for fidgeting, told to sit still when movement was regulated, or shamed for crying when our systems were overwhelmed. Even well-meaning adults often mistook signs of dysregulation for defiance, leaving us to internalize that something was wrong, not just with our behavior, but with our being.

As a result, many of us learned to abandon our bodies. We dissociated, masked, shut down, or lived in our heads, trying to manage our experience cognitively because the body felt unsafe, unreliable, or simply too intense. We became skilled at overriding our signals, pushing through pain, and bracing for impact especially when sensory or emotional overload was constant. This survival strategy may have protected us then. But over time, it created a gap between self and self.

Rebuilding trust with your nervous system is the sacred act of closing that gap. It begins not with control or mastery, but with curiosity. With learning how your unique system speaks, and how it longs to be heard. It is about restoring relationships: with your breath, your gut, your inner yes and no. It's learning to speak the language of your body without fear, judgment, or the need to fix anything.

This chapter is not about eliminating shutdowns or anxiety or overstimulation entirely. That may still happen, because you are living in a world that was not designed for your nervous system. Instead, this chapter invites you to walk with those experiences differently. To become less afraid of your body's responses. To recognize them not as threats, but as messages. And ultimately, to say to your body: *You are not my enemy. You are my oldest companion. I am listening now.*

## Nervous System Practices That Foster Trust and Safety

Rebuilding trust with your nervous system is not a one-time act, it's a lifelong relationship. Especially for neurodivergent people, whose systems may be more reactive, more sensitive, or more easily overwhelmed, nervous system care must be adaptive, respectful, and individualized. Below are some entry points that can help reweave the thread of connection.

### 1. Micro-Tracking: Learning Your Body's Signals

Many neurodivergent people are taught to ignore bodily cues. Micro-tracking is the gentle art of tuning in to what your system is communicating without needing to fix or judge. It can look like:
- Noticing subtle shifts in breath, posture, or temperature.
- Becoming aware of tension patterns (jaw clenching, hand fidgeting, etc.).
- Asking: *What am I sensing? What am I needing?*

The goal isn't constant vigilance, it's reconnection. Over time, this builds somatic fluency and helps you recognize stress patterns before they escalate.

### 2. Creating Sensory Sanctuaries

Because the nervous system is often dysregulated by the environment, curating a sensory-safe space can be profoundly regulating. Consider:

- Wearing preferred textures or fabrics.
- Adjusting light (soft, indirect, or colored).
- Using scent (lavender, frankincense, or another grounding aroma).
- Creating "retreat spaces" at home with sound-dampening tools or cocooning options (blankets, headphones, soft chairs).

Your space becomes a co-regulator, not just a backdrop.

### 3. Movement That Matches Your Nervous System State

Not all movements are helpful in every state. When dysregulated, the key is to match movement to your current nervous system need:

- In freeze or shutdown: slow rocking, gentle stretching, or rhythmic drumming can begin to thaw the system without overwhelm.
- In fight or flight: brisk walking, shaking, dancing, or bouncing can help discharge excess energy and bring grounding.

Movement doesn't need to be formal. It just needs to feel like relief.

### 4. Co-Regulation with Safe Others

Many neurodivergent individuals have experienced relational trauma, especially around expression, pacing, or meltdown responses. Safe co-regulation can be deeply healing. This might include:

- Sitting in silence with a trusted friend.
- Engaging in side-by-side activities that don't require constant talking (puzzles, crafting, gaming).
- Being with animals who respond to your natural rhythms without judgment.

The presence of non-demanding companionship can calm a dysregulated system without the pressure to perform or mask.

### 5. Slowness as a Nervous System Practice

The modern world demands speed. The neurodivergent body often thrives on slowness or having a consistent pace.

Try:

- Deliberate transitions between tasks (e.g., three slow breaths before and after phone use).
- "Pause rituals" to reset between environments.
- Allowing longer lead time to prepare for or recover from social interaction.
- Slowness isn't laziness, it's medicine.

## Why This Work is Sacred

Rebuilding trust with your nervous system isn't just about feeling better, it's about reclaiming your birthright to feel *safe* in your own being. It's about unlearning the lie that regulation must come through suppression. It's about telling the child within you: *I will not abandon you again.*

This work is deeply spiritual. Your body carries not only stress, but wisdom. Not only patterns, but potential. Each moment you pause to ask, "*What do I need?*", you are repairing something generational. Each time you respond with kindness, you say to your nervous system, "You are no longer alone."

## Meet Luke

Luke is a late-diagnosed autistic and gifted man in his early 50s, spent most of his life feeling like his body was betraying him. As a child, he was told to "toughen up" when textures made him wince or when lights and sounds brought him to the brink of tears. He learned to override his discomfort and to survive first in school, then in work, and finally in his relationships. He presented himself calmly, but inside he was often panicked. His body didn't feel like a home. It felt like a landmine.

By midlife, Luke's shutdowns were growing more frequently. After minor stressors, he'd lose language. He'd retreat for days, unable to tolerate even the sound of his own breathing. Despite years of cognitive therapy, he couldn't "think" his way into regulation. What he needed was a new relationship with his nervous system, one rooted in compassion, not control.

Luke's healing began with what he called "micro-consent." He started asking his body small questions and honored the answers:
- Do you want to move or rest right now?
- Would soft lighting help?
- Is this food bringing comfort or confusion?

He discovered his body wasn't the problem, it was the ignored narrator of his life. The more he listened, the more he noticed subtle cues that preceded shutdowns. Tension behind his eyes. A tightening in his chest. A shift in temperature. These weren't signs of weakness; they were *invitations to intervene gently* before collapse.

Luke began building in transition rituals: breathing with a weighted blanket between work and social time; placing his hand on his heart before answering emails; lighting a scented candle to mark the end of the day. Over time, he stopped fearing his dysregulation and started forming an alliance with it. His body wasn't perfect, but it was no longer foreign. It was a place he could live in again.

## Reflection Questions

1. When in your life did you first begin to distrust your body's signals? What shaped that disconnection?

2. What does your body feel like when it is approaching shutdown, meltdown, or overwhelm? What are your early cues?

3. Where in your environment do you feel most regulated and safe? Why?

4. What small practices (rituals, movements, sensory tools) help your nervous system feel supported?

5. What would it mean for your body to become a place of belonging, not just survival?

CHAPTER 39

# DESIGNING A LIFE THAT HONORS YOUR ENERGY

The world is structured around external rhythms 9 to 5 workdays, 40-hour weeks, endless notifications, and relentless forward motion. For those of us who are gifted and neurodivergent, these rhythms often feel foreign, even punishing at times. We are cyclical beings who are sensitive, deep and dynamic. We may move in bursts of brilliance followed by a deep need for rest. Our creativity doesn't clock in. Our nervous systems do not reset on command.

Yet, many of us spend years, decades even, trying to fit into a life designed by and for other people's energy and agendas. We push through fatigue. We override signals. We convince ourselves that exhaustion is just the price of being a "functioning adult." But the truth is simpler and far more radical: You were never meant to live a life that drains you. You were meant to design a life that *honors* your energy.

**Energy Is Information**

In my mentoring practice, I often say that energy isn't just a resource, it's a language. It tells you what aligns and what depletes. When we learn to read and trust our energetic cues, we begin to reclaim a powerful form of inner authority.

Start by noticing:
- When do you feel most alive, focused, and present?
- When do you start to fade or feel agitated, foggy, or numb?

- Which people, environments, and tasks leave you energized and which ones leave you drained?

These are not incidental observations. They are the raw materials for redesigning your life.

Many neurodivergent adults have internalized the belief that their energy is unreliable or "too much" too erratic, too intense, too fragile. But your energy isn't wrong. What's wrong is a society that demands constancy from nervous systems that are meant to ebb and flow.

## The Power of Alignment

Designing a life that honors your energy doesn't mean avoiding responsibility. It means *aligning your responsibilities with your design.* It means asking: *How can I do what I need to do in a way that feels supportive instead of punishing?*

## Alignment might look like:
- Working in sprints instead of forcing 8-hour blocks of focus
- Creating buffer time between social events or meetings
- Building in recovery days after deep emotional or creative output
- Releasing the pressure to respond immediately to every request
- Allowing your body to guide your schedule, not just your calendar

It also means releasing the myth that rest must be earned. Rest is part of the rhythm. It's where integration, insight, and recalibration happen.

When you begin to honor your energy instead of resisting it, you stop working *against* yourself. You become your own collaborator instead of your own taskmaster.

## Listening to the Body's Clock

Your nervous system has a clock, but it may not match the cultural one. Some of us are most focused at night. Others need more transition time in the morning. Some thrive with long periods of solitude;

others need sensory regulation built into their day. This isn't laziness or dysfunction. This is *bio-intelligence*.

Designing a life around your energy requires unlearning the story that productivity is about endurance. True productivity, soul-aligned productivity, comes from *flow*, not force.

### Living the Design: Practices for Energy Alignment

- Track your energy for one week. When are you most alert, creative, or social? When do you crash? Let this data guide your schedule.
- Color-code your calendar by energy intensity: red for high-output, blue for recovery, green for creative flow. This helps you balance your week with awareness.
- Create energy rituals for transitions, grounding before socializing, unwinding after focused work, centering before sleep.
- Build white space into your day. Empty time is not wasted time, it's where restoration and insight live.
- Redefine "enough." Meeting your needs *is* productive. Feeling connected to yourself *is* success.

### Designing from the Inside Out

Most of us were taught to build our lives around expectations and squeeze our energy in after. This chapter is your invitation to reverse the order.

What if you began with your energy, your sensory needs, your rhythms, your sensitivities, and built the rest of your life *around* that? This isn't self-indulgent. It's self-honoring.

When you live in alignment with your energy, you don't just feel better, you *become more of yourself*. Your presence becomes clearer. Your creativity sharpens. Your soul feels heard. And in that space of wholeness, you can do your work, love your people, and move through the world with greater clarity and ease.

Your life is allowed to fit you.

**Meet Chuck**
Chuck spent most of his adult life pushing past his limits. As a gifted systems analyst and self-described "high-functioning introvert," he had built a reputation for being reliable, thorough, and always available. His calendar was a tightly packed grid of meetings, projects, and obligations. Rest was something he scheduled like a chore and even then, he usually skipped it.

Underneath the competence was a man running on fumes. Chuck had lived for decades under the belief that value came from output. Raised in a family where hard work was praised and sensitivity was misunderstood; he learned early on to suppress his internal rhythms. His ADHD went undiagnosed until his early 50s, and by then he had mastered the art of overcompensation. He masked his overwhelm with humor, deflected his exhaustion with caffeine, and explained away his irritability as "just being busy."

The turning point came during a team offsite. After a string of intense days, Chuck found himself completely shut down mentally foggy, emotionally flat, and unable to focus. A colleague noticed his change in demeanor and asked a simple question that stopped him in his tracks: *"What would your work look like if it supported your actual energy instead of demanding you override it?"* Chuck didn't have an answer. But that question lodged itself inside him and refused to leave.

Over the next several months, Chuck began to track his energy patterns not through apps or optimization hacks, but by tuning into his body. He noticed how he peaked mid-morning and needed solitude in the early afternoon. He realized that social engagements drained him faster than he admitted, and that noise sensitivity made open offices nearly unbearable. He discovered that he thought more clearly when walking than sitting, and that even short bursts of natural light dramatically improved his mood.

With guidance, he began to design a rhythm that aligned with these truths. He restructured his calendar, blocking sacred windows of deep-focus time. He started declining back-to-back meetings. He added short movement breaks between tasks, shifted his meals to support blood sugar stability, and stopped apologizing for needing recovery time after social events. It wasn't about doing less; it was about doing differently.

Chuck's productivity actually improved and more importantly, so did his sense of overall wellbeing. He stopped collapsing at the end of the day. He began to feel a quiet pride in honoring his energy instead of resenting it. His nervous system softened. His creativity returned. His presence with others deepened because he was no longer running on empty.

Today, Chuck is the same brilliant analyst and now he's also a man who chooses his own rhythm. A man who listens. A man who no longer believes that exhaustion is a badge of honor.

**Reflection Questions**

1. What are the natural energy patterns of your body and mind and how do they conflict or align with your current lifestyle?

2. What people, environments, or activities consistently drain you and which ones restore or energize you?

3. What cultural or internalized beliefs have made you feel guilty about resting or working differently?

4. What would your days look like if they were built around your energy instead of expectations?

5. What's one small change you can make this week to honor your true rhythm, even in the midst of obligations?

## CHAPTER 40

# CHOOSING A LIFE YOU DON'T HAVE TO RECOVER FROM

For the neurodivergent soul, energy is not a limitless resource, it is a sacred current. Yet so often, we are taught to manage our lives as though we are machines with an "on" switch. Our society celebrates constant output and punishes rest. It rewards quick responses, packed calendars, and high visibility. But for many neurodivergent individuals, this is not just exhausting, it is unsustainable.

We are not lazy. We are *cyclical*. Our energy may rise in creative bursts and drop into stillness without warning. We may need longer to recover from social engagement, transitions, or decision-making. We may experience deep joy and insight, but only if we're not being asked to override our inner rhythms.

Designing a life that honors your energy is not about perfect scheduling or self-optimization. It's about *liberation*. It's the radical act of building a life that is responsive to your actual nervous system, not to the expectations of others. It means releasing the shame around needing slowness, solitude, or extra space. It means letting go of the "shoulds" and leaning into what is genuinely life-giving.

This chapter is about crafting a daily life that doesn't require constant recovery. It's about choosing sustainable joy over burnout, deep focus over hyper-productivity, and embodied alignment over performance. You are not here to prove your worth through exhaustion. You are here to live in rhythm with your soul.

## Ways to Design a Life That Honors Your Energy

Neurodivergent energy is precious. It is also highly sensitive to context. The following principles are not prescriptions but invitations to explore what would shift if your life was built *with* your nervous system instead of against it.

### 1. Map Your Rhythms (and Stop Fighting Them)

Your energy has a shape, a texture, and depth. Learn it.

Try tracking:
- Times of day when you feel most alert, grounded, or focused.
- Times when you feel most easily overstimulated, scattered, or fatigued.
- The impact of food, light, noise, and interaction on your body.

Once you understand your pattern, you can build on it, doing deep work when you're high-energy, and reserving low-energy times for rest or simple tasks. This is energetic intelligence.

### 2. Build Recovery into Your Routine

Recovery is not optional. It is part of the cycle.

Create space:
- After social events, even if they're enjoyable.
- After overstimulation (errands, travel, digital overload).
- Between transitions give yourself "buffer zones" to recalibrate.

Recovery might look like solitude, nature time, body movement, naps, or no-input time (no sound, no screen, no task). The key is to *expect* the need not treat it like a surprise or weakness.

### 3. Design Environments That Feed, Not Drain

Your environment is either nourishing you or taking from your energy. Consider:
- Noise levels and auditory input.

- Visual clutter and lighting.
- Accessibility of tools, sensory supports, or calming rituals.
- Workspaces that invite focus and ease, not just functionality.

Creating aligned spaces is not indulgence. It's energy stewardship.

### 4. Say No as a Form of Sacred Protection

Saying no is not rejection, it is selection. Choosing what supports your energy also means protecting it from unnecessary depletion.

Learn to say:
- "Let me check my energy and get back to you."
- "I can't commit to that but thank you for thinking of me."
- "That's not aligned with my bandwidth right now."

Let your "no" be a yes to your sustainability.

### 5. Create a Rhythm of Joy and Meaning

Life that honors your energy isn't just about reducing overwhelm, it's about *building delight*. Regularly include:
- Sensory joy (a favorite sound, texture, scent).
- Creative play, even without a productive outcome.
- Deep work or "flow time" in your passion areas.
- Moments of awe or wonder.

These become your inner scaffolding, anchoring you through intensity or change.

### This is Your Life. You Are Allowed to Design It Differently.

You do not have to hustle for permission to live in a way that makes sense to you. You are not broken because you need more rest, more quiet, more space between things. You are wise for listening to your limits. You are whole enough to choose what honors your body, your mind, your heart.

There is no universal blueprint for an energy-honoring life but there *is* a deeply personal one, written into your being. Your job is to follow its signals. To shape your days like sacred containers. To choose what sustains you. And to believe, with your whole nervous system, that this gentler way is not failure. It is freedom.

## Meet Avery

Avery is a gifted nonbinary adult with ADHD and sensory processing sensitivity who used to live in a near-constant state of energetic depletion. They had internalized a belief that in order to be taken seriously as a professional, as an artist, as a neurodivergent person they had to "do it all." Their calendar was a patchwork of overcommitment. Their days were filled with meetings, errands, emotional caretaking, and bursts of hyperfocus followed by days of crash.

Eventually, Avery hit a wall. A shutdown that lasted weeks. They lost interest in everything. Their body ached. Their mind was foggy. What began as burnout became an existential crisis. *If I can't sustain this pace,* they thought, *then who am I?*

Avery's turning point came not with a dramatic epiphany, but a single act of honesty: admitting they were tired of performing someone else's version of "success." They started by tracking energy patterns over a few weeks when they felt most alive, when they crashed, when their body said no. They discovered their most creative time was early morning, but they were often spending those hours scrolling or responding to emails.

So, they began to restructure. They blocked off 8–10am for writing and movement. They scheduled social time only after restful buffers. They moved errands to the middle of the week to avoid weekend crowds. They created a "recovery margin" after overstimulating events a half-day to decompress, not just 10 minutes. Their life became quieter, yes, but also fuller. They began to feel pleasure again. The color came back to their world.

## Reflection Questions

1. What daily or weekly patterns currently leave you feeling drained, and what would feel more supportive instead?

2. What time of day do you feel most alive, creative, or clear and how might you protect that window?

3. What sensory, social, or environmental inputs tend to drain you, and which ones restore you?

4. What boundaries do you need to set (with others or yourself) to better protect your energy?

5. If you could design your days based on your own rhythms, what would shift? What would be possible then?

# CHAPTER 41

# THE SACRED ACT OF UNMASKING

Peeling back your many layers of protection is paramount to your happiness and wellbeing. Fitting in is not the goal. It never was. From our earliest moments, we were conditioned to believe that sameness is safety. We were taught to flatten our edges, to silence our knowing, to dim the brilliance that made others uncomfortable. For neurodivergent souls, especially those who are gifted, intuitive, or highly sensitive masking became a means of survival. Not a choice. A necessity.

The mask formed early. Sometimes it looked like people-pleasing. Other times, silence. Perfectionism. Overachievement. Avoidance. Hyperawareness. Each layer carefully placed to protect us from a world that didn't understand how we moved, felt, thought, or sensed.

Masking served a purpose. Let's honor that. It helped us survive systems that were not designed with us in mind. It helped us stay safe in families, schools, relationships, and workplaces that rewarded conformity and punished difference. It was smart. It was resourceful. It was sacred in its own way.

Still there comes a time when the cost becomes too high. The longer we wear the mask, the more disconnected we become from our own essence. We start to question what is real and what is performance. We begin to mistake adaptation for identity. The very strategies that once helped us cope start to silence our soul.

Unmasking is the moment we stop asking, "How do I need to

show up in order to be to be accepted? You will want to begin asking, "Who am I when I am not performing for acceptance"? This is about remembrance, remembering who you authentically are, free of others' expectations and definitions of who you should be. This process is about choosing truth over habit, one small moment at a time. You do not need or want to dismantle your entire life and perceived identity markers overnight or by the end of the weekend. You can let your body exhale when you stop pretending. Letting your voice come through without polishing it to be palatable. Letting your rhythm guide you, not the pressure to keep up.

Unmasking is a sacred act of returning. You are not becoming someone new. You are reuniting with the self you've always been beneath the layers of adaptation. This process may be slow. It may be emotional. It may stretch your nervous system. That's okay. Go gently. Meet each piece of yourself with compassion, not critique.

There may be places in your life where unmasking doesn't yet feel safe. Honor that. You don't owe your authenticity to every space. Self-betrayal is not a requirement for connection. Discernment is part of the practice. Unmasking is not an all-or-nothing act it is a sacred unfolding. And you get to decide the pace.

Start by noticing the places where your breath shortens. Where your laughter is forced. Where your voice feels like it belongs to someone else. These are invitations. Invitations to come home.

**Moving Forward with Unmasking**
Unmasking is not a task to complete. It is a lifelong rhythm. It asks for presence, not performance. It asks for courage, not perfection. You will discover parts of yourself that feel unfamiliar at first. That's part of the beauty. Let them emerge slowly. Let them surprise you. Let them return you to your aliveness.

When you unmask, you make space for real connection. Not just with others, but with the sacred core of your own being. You begin to feel safe in your own presence. And from that place, life begins to shift. The relationships that can hold your truth begin to form.

The environments that suffocate you fall away. Your inner voice gets louder. Your soul feels heard. This is the path of liberation. not because it's easy, but because it's real. Not because it's quick, but because it's true. So, when your body says, *this is me,* Listen. When your soul whispers, *I want to be known,* let it speak. And when the mask begins to loosen, let it fall. You are not too much. You are not a burden. You are not wrong. You are worthy of being seen unfiltered, unpolished, and fully alive.

## Meet Lila

Lila is a gifted woman in her early 40s who had always been the "quiet one" in her family and community. As a child, she was told she was "too sensitive" and "too intense." She learned to suppress her thoughts, hide her emotions, and wear a facade of calmness to avoid scrutiny. This masking became second nature to her as she moved into adulthood, even though it left her feeling isolated and disconnected.

Lila worked as a teacher, a profession that required constant interaction with students and parents. Over the years, she had perfected the art of wearing the mask. She was the "model teacher" , always composed, always polite, always on top of everything. But inside, she was exhausted, overwhelmed, and struggling with feelings of inadequacy. She had become a caricature of herself.

It wasn't until Lila had a burnout after a particularly difficult year that she realized something had to change. During her recovery, she began to notice the moments when she felt most alive, most herself. They were often the small, seemingly insignificant moments, like when she allowed herself to be a little messy in the classroom, or when she shared her love of poetry with a colleague. She realized that when she let her guard down, when she was willing to show her true self, she felt more connected and alive.

Lila began to experiment with unmasking in small ways. She allowed herself to laugh louder, to speak more freely, to share her opinions without worrying about being judged. She started to dress in clothes that felt more like "her" looser, more comfortable, and expressive of her true style. She began to set firmer boundaries at work, saying "no" when she needed to, and asking for help when she felt overwhelmed.

The process wasn't easy. It was messy and uncomfortable, and it required vulnerability. But little by little, Lila began to feel more authentic. The mask that had once protected her now felt like a burden she was ready to let go of. The more she embraced her true self, the more she found a deeper sense of belonging not to the world around her, but to herself.

**Reflection Questions**

1. Where in my life am I still wearing a mask to feel safe, accepted, or understood and what is the cost of continuing to wear it? (Notice the environments, relationships, or roles where you feel the pressure to perform or hide.)

2. What parts of my true self have I been protecting that are now ready to be seen, honored, or reclaimed? (These may include ways you move, speak, think, feel, or create that you've kept tucked away.)

3. How does my body respond when I'm masking, and how does it feel when I allow myself to be fully present and real? (Pay attention to physical sensations like tension, breath, energy, or ease.)

4. In what situations do I feel most free to show up without filtering and what makes those moments possible? (Look for the conditions, people, or environments that support your unmasked self.)

5. What would it look like to take one small step toward unmasking in a way that feels safe, supported, and aligned with my truth? (Let this be an invitation, not a demand. Honor your own pace.)

## CHAPTER 42

# WRITING YOUR OWN DEFINITION OF SUCCESS

From the moment you are born, you are subtly conditioned to follow a predetermined path, one that has been carved out by culture, society, and family expectations. This path, laden with conventional markers of success, academic achievements, career progression, financial wealth, public recognition becomes a shadow that we chase but never quite catch. For many, especially those who are gifted or neurodivergent, this societal blueprint often does not align with your inner truth. It creates a gap between who you are and who you are expected to be. By writing your own definition of success, you reclaim your personal power.

This gap is often filled with dissatisfaction, pressure, and a deep yearning for something more authentic. But breaking free from the conditioning of society, the pressure to conform, and the "one-size-fits-all" definition of success is not an easy task. It requires not only courage but also an active reclaiming of your personal values, your desires, and your own truth.

When you are conditioned to believe that success is based on external accomplishments, having the right job, making the right amount of money, attaining fame, or achieving perfection, you begin to live your life for others' approval. You may end up chasing goals that were never yours, putting your true desires and passions on the back burner.

The sacred act of defining success for yourself is about liberating yourself from this old conditioning. It's about shedding the expectations that no longer serve you and allowing yourself to live a life that resonates with your soul's calling. True success is not about ticking off societal check boxes, it's about living authentically, in alignment with your core values, and embracing the joy that comes from being true to yourself.

**Breaking Free from the Old Conditioning of Success**
To define success on your own terms, you first must deconstruct the old patterns and beliefs that have been ingrained in you since childhood.

Here are some ways to begin freeing yourself from the shackles of societal conditioning:

## 1. Question What You've Been Taught
Many of us have been taught that success is about accumulation of wealth, status, or achievement. Take time to reflect on the messages you received growing up:
- Who taught you about success? What were their values, and how did they shape your beliefs?
- Did they prioritize external achievements, or did they encourage you to cultivate inner fulfillment?
- What aspects of their definition of success feel authentic to you, and which ones do you now question?

The first step is simply questioning the assumptions you've inherited. Awareness is the key to breaking free.

## 2. Let Go of Perfectionism
Society often equates success with perfectionism, the idea that you must excel at everything you do and never show signs of weakness. For many neurodivergent souls, perfectionism becomes an overwhelming burden. The truth is, perfectionism is often a response to the fear of not being "enough," of not measuring up to the standards set by others.

To redefine success, you must release the need to be perfect. Success is not about flawless performance, it's about learning, growing, and aligning with your values. Embrace imperfection as part of the process and allow yourself the grace to evolve without the pressure to achieve perfection at every step.

### 3. Challenge the Idea of "Fitting In"

From an early age, we are taught that to be successful, we must "fit in" with societal norms. But the reality is that true fulfillment doesn't come from blending into the crowd, it comes from standing in your own truth. For neurodivergent individuals, this often means resisting the urge to suppress your unique ways of thinking and being. Instead of striving to fit into the world's mold, consider how you can bring your authentic self into the world.

- How can you honor your unique gifts without trying to conform to someone else's idea of success?
- What would it look like to embrace your individuality instead of suppressing it to fit in?

Success does not require you to blend in; it requires you to stand out by being unapologetically you.

### 4. Unplug from the Comparison Game

Social media and the ever-present visibility of others' lives often contribute to the pressure to measure up. We are constantly bombarded with images of success, perfect careers, flawless families, exotic vacations that create a false narrative of what success should look like. Unplugging from this comparison game is essential for freeing yourself from these unhealthy standards:

- Take breaks from social media or curate your feeds to include only those who inspire you authentically, rather than those who make you feel inadequate.
- Reconnect with your own journey by focusing on your progress rather than comparing it to others.

- Cultivate gratitude for the unique path you are walking, knowing that it is yours and yours alone.

Remember, your success story is one of a kind, don't let someone else's story steal your spotlight.

## 5. Focus on Inner Fulfillment, Not External Validation

When you begin to define success on your terms, you no longer rely on external validation to feel worthy or accomplished. Success is no longer about awards, titles, or praise from others. It becomes about your internal experience, how you feel about your choices, your progress, and the life you're creating. Ask yourself:

- How does success feel in my body? Is it peace, joy, or contentment?
- When I align with my true self, what shifts occur in my life? Do I feel more fulfilled, less stressed, or more at ease?
- What can I do today to move toward a life that fulfills me internally, rather than seeking external rewards?

Your success is not defined by how others see you, but by how you see yourself and the life you're living.

## Reflecting on Your Own Definition of Success

Success is not a destination that can be neatly defined by a society that has its own set of expectations. It is a personal journey, a fluid, evolving process that reflects who you are at the deepest level. It's about crafting a life that feels aligned with your soul's purpose, passions, and desires.

When you liberate yourself from the constraints of conventional success, you allow room for your authentic path to unfold. Success becomes something you define and experience, not something you must achieve through comparison, competition, or external validation. It is an invitation to create a life that truly resonates with you, on your own terms.

In the next section, we will dive into how you can begin to write your own definition of success, one that reflects your core values, intrinsic motivations, and your unique place in the world.

### Practical Ways to Define Success for Yourself

The process of defining your own success is personal, liberating, and transformative. It requires self-reflection, introspection, and an openness to redefining everything you thought you knew about achievement. Here are some practices and exercises to help you start this journey.

### 1. Reflect on External Definitions of Success

To write your own definition of success, it's important to first examine the external definitions you've absorbed. Consider:

- What messages about success did you receive growing up? From your family, school, media, or culture?
- Which of these definitions felt aligned with your soul, and which ones felt like a heavy burden?
- How have these external definitions shaped your sense of self-worth and achievement?

This reflection will help you become aware of the societal pressures you've internalized and create space to develop your own unique standards.

### 2. Identify What Truly Brings You Fulfillment

Success is deeply connected to fulfillment. For many neurodivergent individuals, fulfillment doesn't come from outward accolades or comparisons; it comes from intrinsic satisfaction, deep engagement, and inner peace. Take time to explore what truly nourishes you:

- When do you feel most alive and connected? What activities, relationships, or environments bring you joy?
- What do you love to do that feels expansive and natural, not driven by a desire for recognition?
- What qualities or values do you hold most dear? (Creativity, authenticity, kindness, freedom, connection, etc.)

Write down your answers. These insights are key to defining a version of success that honors your soul's desires.

## 3. Clarify Your Core Values
Success is not just about what you achieve, it's about how you achieve it. Your values are the guiding principles that will shape your path.

Some common values that may resonate with you include:
- Creativity and self-expression
- Peace and inner calm
- Connection and community
- Learning and personal growth
- Health and well-being

Take some time to identify your core values. When you align your definition of success with your values, you create a life that feels deeply meaningful and fulfilling.

## 4. Let Go of the Need for External Validation
Much of our struggle with success comes from seeking approval or validation from others. To rewrite your definition of success, you must free yourself from the need for external approval:
- Ask yourself: What would it look like if I didn't need anyone's validation to feel successful?
- How can I celebrate my wins big or small without waiting for external acknowledgment?
- How can I internalize success, rather than relying on others' opinions of it?

Letting go of external validation allows you to take ownership of your success and build a life that feels deeply personal and empowered.

## 5. Create a Vision of Success That Feels Aligned with Your Heart's Desire
Your definition of success is a vision for your life that reflects who you are, what you value, and how you want to show up in the world.

Consider:

- What does your ideal life look like? What activities, relationships, and environments support your sense of success?
- How do you measure your success? Is it based on personal growth, creativity, health, happiness, or something else?
- How does success feel in your body? Is it a sense of ease, excitement, peace, or purpose?

Write your definition of success as a statement or vision. Keep it flexible, open to change, and free from rigid expectations.

When you begin to write your own definition of success, you free yourself from the exhausting pursuit of someone else's vision. You step into the truth of who you are and allow your life to unfold according to your own terms. Success becomes a reflection of your growth, values, and personal evolution, not a destination you must race toward.

By rejecting external pressures and embracing your unique path, you give yourself the power to shape a life that is deeply meaningful, fulfilling, and true to your soul. You don't have to prove anything. You don't have to follow a prescribed path. You get to choose, and in that choice, you unlock the truest, most powerful version of success you could ever hope to experience.

**Meet Maria**

Maria is a 35-year-old artist with ADHD who had spent most of her adult life following the traditional markers of success: pursuing a prestigious degree, climbing the career ladder, and striving for recognition in the art world. On the surface, her achievements seemed impressive. She had a well-regarded art gallery show, received invitations to exclusive events, and was often praised for her technical skill. Yet, something inside her felt empty. She found herself drained by the constant pressure to produce, to be visible, and to compete with other artists for attention and acclaim. She realized that the art world, as she had known it, was no longer fulfilling her deep creative need. The pursuit of recognition had dimmed her passion for the work itself.

In a moment of reflection, Maria began to question what success truly meant to her. What was her art really for? What did it mean to live a life that was "successful" in her eyes? Through journaling, she uncovered that her true definition of success was not about fame or accolades, it was about the freedom to create on her own terms, to explore new forms of expression, and to connect with others in authentic, meaningful ways.

Maria decided to pivot. She reduced her reliance on external validation, chose to focus on smaller, more intimate art shows, and created a platform for collaborating with other artists who shared her values. She also spent more time in nature, reconnecting with the source of her creative energy, rather than chasing after trends and external measures of success. Over time, Maria discovered that success, for her, was about alignment, joy, and the quiet satisfaction of creating work that felt true to her soul.

**Reflection Questions**

1. How have external definitions of success shaped your life and choices? Which of these definitions no longer serve you?

2. What activities, environments, or experiences make you feel truly fulfilled, alive, and connected?

3. What are your core values, and how do they inform your vision of success?

4. What would it look like if you no longer sought external validation for your success? How could you celebrate your achievements without relying on others' opinions?

5. Write your own definition of success. What does success mean to you now, in this season of your life?

# CHAPTER 43

# THE PRACTICE OF SELF-COMPASSION

For the gifted and neurodivergent soul, self-compassion can feel elusive, even unnatural. Many of us were praised for what we could *do*, not for who we *are*. We learned to measure our value in terms of productivity, intellect, emotional control, or uniqueness. And when we struggled, as all humans do, we often internalized blame rather than receiving care.

Self-compassion invites us into a different relationship with ourselves. One where we don't have to earn kindness. One where pain is met with tenderness, not punishment. One where we stop abandoning ourselves at the exact moment, we need our own presence most.

Self-compassion is not a feeling. It is a daily practice. And for those of us who are deeply sensitive, deeply wired, and deeply self-aware, it is often the practice that allows everything else to begin healing.

## Why It Feels So Hard

Many neurodivergent individuals are deeply empathic. We offer care, patience, and understanding to others with great ease, but turn inward and find only self-criticism or avoidance. This isn't because we're unkind. It's because many of us were never modeled on what a compassionate self-relationship looks like.

We were taught:
- Push through it.
- Don't be so dramatic.

- You should know better.
- Be strong. Be better. Be less sensitive.

Over time, these messages eventually form an inner dialogue, a critical narrator that is always bracing, always correcting, never quite satisfied. The soul gets muffled beneath a constant pressure to be "more" or "better."

In my mentoring practice, I often meet brilliant, thoughtful adults who show up for others beautifully, but have no idea how to stay with themselves through difficulty. They know how to fix, but not how to feel. They know how to achieve, but not how to attune.

Self-compassion bridges this gap. It teaches us to stay.

## What Self-Compassion Actually Is

Self-compassion is not indulgence. It is not a luxury or a fallback plan for when everything else fails. It is the foundation for emotional resilience, nervous system regulation, and authentic self-trust. For the neurodivergent soul, it is oxygen.

At its core, self-compassion has three essential elements: self-kindness, a sense of common humanity, and mindful awareness. These are not abstract ideals. They are practices, learnable, repeatable, life-giving.

Self-kindness is the decision to relate to yourself with warmth instead of judgment. It is what happens when, instead of asking "What's wrong with me?" you ask, "What do I need right now?" It is allowing yourself to pause when you are overwhelmed, to soothe rather than scold when you struggle. Self-kindness interrupts the internalized narratives that say you must be harder, faster, better, or quieter to belong.

The second pillar, remembering your common humanity, is especially healing for gifted and neurodivergent individuals who often carry an invisible grief: the grief of being *the only one*. Many of us grow up believing we are fundamentally different, too much, too intense, or not enough in some essential way. Self-compassion says: you are not broken; you are human. And every human being knows what it's like to struggle, to fall short, to yearn for connection. You are not alone in your pain, nor are you alone in your worth.

The third piece is mindfulness, the gentle awareness of what is happening within you, without over-identifying or turning away. Mindfulness allows you to be with your inner experience rather than buried by it. It makes space for clarity, for witnessing your emotions and thoughts with curiosity instead of shame. For the neurodivergent mind, which may feel bombarded by stimuli or caught in rapid emotional cycles, mindfulness is an anchoring rope a way to come home to yourself again and again.

There is one more ingredient I believe is essential for neurodivergent self-compassion and it is giving yourself inner permission to express your differences without apology. This means giving yourself the freedom to stim, to take a longer pause, to communicate in your own rhythm, to opt out of environments that overwhelm your senses, and to lean into your special interests with joy rather than self-consciousness. It means accepting that the ways you move through the world may not match the norm and allowing that to be okay, even beautiful. After all, you are different by design and matching the norm may not be what you are meant to bring to the world.

To be self-compassionate is to say to yourself, "I am allowed to be who I am. I am allowed to be different by design". It's the daily act of choosing presence over performance, gentleness over grit, and authenticity over assimilation.

You don't have to wait until you are less sensitive, more productive, or easier to understand to be worthy of love, especially from yourself. Let this be your permission slip. Let this be the moment you breathe deeper. Let this be the beginning of a new relationship with yourself. Your time to thrive is now.

## How Self-compassion Sounds in Practice

Self-compassion might sound like:
- "It makes sense that this feels hard for me."
- "I don't have to get this perfect. I just need to stay connected."

- "I've been trying so hard. Maybe I deserve some gentleness right now."
- "This moment doesn't define my worth."

It might look like:
- Placing your hand over your heart and breathing deeply.
- Letting yourself cry without trying to stop it.
- Taking a break before you're completely drained.
- Replacing inner judgment with inner witnessing.

These are small acts. They can change everything. These are a few good ideas. I encourage you to try different strategies and do what resonates for you.

## Building the Practice

Self-compassion grows through repetition. You will not do this practice perfectly. This is where self-compassion and self-forgiveness are vital to your health and wellbeing. You don't have to get it "right." You just have to *begin*.

## Here are a few practices you can explore:

**The Mirror Pause:** Each morning or evening, look at yourself in the mirror and speak a kind phrase aloud. Even if it feels awkward. Even if your voice shakes. Start with: "I'm learning to be gentle with you."

**Name the Inner Child:** When you notice harsh self-talk, pause and ask: *Would I say this to a child I love?* Then speak to yourself as you would to them.

**Body Gratitude Scan:** At the end of the day, thank your body. Even if it struggled. Even if it didn't meet your expectations. "Thank you, hands, for everything you carried. Thank you, heart, for staying open."

**Compassionate Journaling:** Write a letter to yourself from the perspective of someone who loves you unconditionally. Let that voice speak to the parts of you that are hurting.

You do not have to earn your right to be gentle with yourself. You are allowed to need grace. You are allowed to hold yourself tenderly. Your sensitivity is not the enemy of strength; it is the gateway to wisdom. And self-compassion is not an extra, it is the foundation.

This practice, more than any other, will teach you how to come home to yourself.

**Meet José**

José was the kind of person others often described as "driven." A gifted entrepreneur in his early 40s, he had built a thriving consultancy and was known for solving complex problems with speed and precision. On the outside, he appeared confident, charismatic, and composed. On the inside, he carried a storm of self-judgment.

From childhood, José had internalized the idea that success was the only acceptable expression of his worth. Anything less than excellence felt like failure. He was hard on himself—not just about his work, but about his emotions, his ADHD-fueled distractions, his sensitivity to sound and light, his social fatigue. When he couldn't keep up with his own impossible standards, he spiraled into harsh self-talk: *You're lazy. You're falling behind. You should be able to handle this.*

It wasn't until a trusted mentor gently asked him, "What would happen if you spoke to yourself like someone you loved?" that something cracked open. The question haunted him—in a good way. He realized he had never once considered compassion as a tool for growth. Criticism had always been his fuel.

José began to explore self-compassion not as an abstract concept, but as a daily practice. At first, it felt awkward. He resisted the softness, worried that if he eased up, he'd become complacent. But with time, he discovered that self-compassion didn't diminish his ambition, it refined it.

Instead of pushing through burnout, José began pausing to check in with his body. Instead of berating himself for a missed deadline, he acknowledged his humanity and adjusted his pace. When he caught himself spiraling into shame, he started asking: *What am I needing right now?*

He noticed that when he treated himself with kindness, his creativity flowed more freely. His relationships deepened. He no longer needed to prove his value in every room because he had begun to internalize it.

One of the most powerful moments in his journey came during a late-night journaling session, when he wrote: "I forgive myself for being a human learning how to love himself". That sentence became a mantra, a new baseline.

José still strives, still dreams big, but he no longer ties his worth to constant achievement. He practices self-compassion as a daily devotion: through mindful breaks, intentional language, and moments of breath-filled presence. He knows now that strength isn't found in harshness it's found in the courage to offer himself grace, especially when it's hardest to do so.

## Reflection Questions

1. In what ways have you been taught to earn your worth through performance or perfection? How might self-kindness challenge that narrative?

2. When have you felt most alone in your struggles? Can you begin to see your experience as part of our shared human journey not proof of brokenness, but proof of being human?

3. What's one area in your life where mindfulness pausing to notice without judgment might help you relate to yourself with more gentleness?

4. Where in your life are you still waiting for permission to be different? What might shift if you gave yourself that permission today?

5. Imagine speaking to your younger self at a moment when you felt overwhelmed or misunderstood. What words of self-compassion would you offer?

# CHAPTER 44

# BELONGING TO YOURSELF

For many gifted and neurodivergent souls, life begins with a search for belonging and often that search is outward. We try to belong to peer groups, institutions, systems, even family dynamics that ask us to shrink, mask, or override our true nature. We learn to monitor ourselves, edit our tone, suppress our instincts. We bend in the name of being chosen. And yet, despite our best efforts, we often still feel like outsiders. The deeper truth is this: *no external belonging can ever replace the experience of belonging to yourself.*

Belonging to yourself is not about isolation or self-sufficiency. It is about *homecoming.* It is the sacred process of choosing your own presence. Of learning to sit with yourself in love rather than scrutiny. Of building a relationship with your inner world that is rooted in acceptance rather than adaptation.

For the neurodivergent person, whose way of being may challenge conventional norms, this kind of self-belonging is not just healing, it is *liberation.*

**The Cost of Conditional Belonging**
Many of us learned early that certain parts of ourselves were "too much," "too sensitive," "too intense," or "too different" to be accepted. So we camouflaged. We became excellent at reading the room, decoding unspoken rules, and morphing to match the expectations around us.

But conditional belonging always comes with a cost: you cannot be fully loved if you are not fully seen. When belonging is dependent on performance, agreement, or masking, what we gain in approval, we lose in authenticity. Over time, this fractures our sense of self. We become homesick for something we've never quite known.

In my mentoring practice, I've worked with many brilliant adults who've spent their lives belonging *everywhere and nowhere*. They've earned the praise of colleagues, the admiration of peers, even the affection of others, yet still feel invisible. What they are missing is not connection. It's self-connection.

## Your Return Home

Belonging to yourself is a slow, sacred return. It is the decision to stop abandoning yourself, especially when things get hard.

It looks like:
- Trusting your desires and preferences, even when they seem inconvenient to others.
- Honoring your sensory needs without apology.
- Saying no, even if it disappoints someone.
- Saying yes, even if it doesn't make sense to anyone but you.
- Listening to your inner voice when the world is shouting its opinion.
- Being willing to disappoint others rather than betray yourself.

This is not selfishness. This is soul stewardship. When you belong to yourself, you create a solid ground beneath your feet. You become a safe place for your own sensitivity, complexity, and evolving truth. And paradoxically, from this place of self-rootedness, *true connection with others becomes more possible.*

You're no longer performing to be loved. You are showing up as someone who *already knows* they are lovable.

## Your Practice of Gentle Reclamation

Belonging to yourself doesn't require perfection. It requires presence.

You might begin with simple check-ins:
- What do I need right now, that I've been overriding?
- Where have I been outsourcing my sense of okay-ness?

- What would it feel like to show up for myself here?

Let your body lead. Let your breath return to you. Let your inner world become a place you are not afraid to visit. This is the work of unmasking, yes, but also of releasing shame. You do not need to prove anything to earn your own belonging. You are already worthy of being with yourself. You are already enough.

Belonging to yourself is the foundation of every other kind of belonging. When you are rooted in your truth, you no longer beg for space, you occupy it with quiet dignity. You no longer contort to be loved; you radiate from a place of inner knowing. You are not too much. You are not broken. You are not behind. You are worthy of your own company. You are worthy of your own care. You are worthy of coming home.

**Meet Nicholas**

Nicholas is a 38-year-old systems engineer who had mastered the art of blending in. Diagnosed late in life with both ADHD and sensory processing sensitivity, he had spent years trying to "pass" as neurotypical in corporate environments that prized conformity over creativity. He was admired for his brilliance and efficiency but often felt like he was cosplaying a version of himself just to survive.

Growing up, Nicholas had internalized the belief that in order to be accepted, he had to minimize his complexity. He quieted his curiosity, filtered his emotions, and edited his voice in conversations. When he showed up authentically, the feedback was often some version of: tone it down. The pain of rejection led him to become hyper-adaptable. He wore masks so well that even he began to forget what lived underneath them.

It wasn't until a health breakdown forced him into extended medical leave that things began to unravel and finally, reweave. Removed from the relentless pressure to perform, Nicholas felt the first stirrings of something unfamiliar: the desire to feel safe in his own presence.

He began therapy and enrolled in a neurodivergent men's circle, where for the first time in his adult life, he didn't have to translate his experience. Slowly, gently, he began to unmask. He paid attention to the texture of his days. He noticed which environments drained him, which ones nourished him. He started setting small boundaries, practicing sensory kindness, and telling the truth in places he used to smile and nod.

One afternoon, while sitting on his porch with a cup of tea, Nicholas had a realization that brought him to tears: "I've spent my whole life trying to belong to everyone else. I never learned how to belong to me".

That moment became a hinge point. He started writing again something he had loved as a child but abandoned in favor of more "practical" paths. He stopped forcing himself into social situations that left him depleted. He gave himself permission to want what he wanted without judgment. And he learned to trust his not as much as his yes.

Nicholas still works in tech, but now he leads with transparency and builds his schedule around his sensory and cognitive rhythms. He doesn't attend every meeting. He doesn't say yes out of guilt. Most importantly, he doesn't leave himself behind. He is no longer trying to earn a seat at someone else's table. He has built his own.

**Reflection Questions**

1. Where in your life have you traded authenticity for acceptance and how has that impacted your sense of self?

2. What parts of you have been silenced or suppressed in the name of fitting in? Are you ready to welcome them home?

3. What does it feel like in your body when you are in alignment with self-belonging? How do you recognize that state?

4. What would change if you no longer needed anyone else's approval to be at peace with yourself?

5. What's one small act you can take this week that reinforces your commitment to belonging to yourself first?

## CHAPTER 45

# YOU ARE DOING THE WORK, RECEIVE THE LIFE YOU IMAGINE

You are doing the work. We've all been taught to believe that success is something we must *earn, that* it's something that only comes after endless sacrifice, tireless effort, and a constant, never-ending hustle. The world tells us that in order to receive, we must work harder, go further, push through obstacles, and overcome each challenge as it comes. But what if success, fulfillment, and peace aren't about *doing more*? What if they are about *becoming*, becoming the person who is open and ready to receive the life they've long imagined?

I want you to pause for a moment and truly acknowledge this: you have already been engaged in deep transformative work. You have been showing up for yourself, day after day, even when the journey seemed endless, even when it felt like you were walking uphill in the face of doubt. Whether you realize it or not, you've been cultivating change from the inside out, transforming the patterns that once held you back, healing the wounds of the past, and bravely redefining what success means to you. This work may not always be visible to the outside world, but it is profound, sacred, and foundational to the life that is waiting for you.

The work of healing, of unlearning old narratives, of letting go of what no longer serves you, of honoring your own rhythms and needs, this is the work you've been doing. The labor of releasing trauma, of questioning societal expectations, of reclaiming your worth and dignity this is the work. And it is no small feat. This work is a triumph in itself, a revolution of the soul, one that has shaped you and brought you to this exact moment.

Now, it is time for you to understand something crucial: You are not here to endlessly struggle, fight, and work in the name of worthiness.

You are worthy *right now*. Your value is not defined by how much you accomplish or how hard you work. Your value is inherent in your very being. The life you have imagined, the life you deserve, is not something to chase after; it is something to *receive*. The seeds have been planted; the foundation has been set. It is time to step into a state of openness, of receiving because everything you have worked for, everything you have been preparing for, is already making its way to you.

**A Shift in Perspective: Moving from "Doing" to "Receiving"**

As a neurodivergent soul, you have likely spent much of your life trying to prove yourself either to meet the world's expectations, to meet the expectations of others, or even to meet the expectations you have internalized about yourself. This striving, this perpetual effort to be "enough," can be exhausting, and it often leaves little room for receiving the gifts that life is ready to offer. There is a profound truth I want you to internalize: You do not have to earn your life. You are not a machine, and you have inherent value. With each breath, you are receiving the gift of life.

You do not have to strive endlessly to prove that you are worthy of love, peace, success, and fulfillment. The truth is you were born worthy of all these things. The work you've done, whether it's healing old wounds, redefining your beliefs, or simply showing up as your authentic self has already set you on the path of receiving. Now, it is about releasing the need to constantly prove your worth through doing, and instead, opening your heart to the possibility of receiving what you have already worked to create.

You have spent years cultivating growth and understanding, often in ways that no one else could see. Now, the time has come for you to release the idea that life must be earned through struggle. You are ready to step into a space where you allow life to come to you not because you have earned it, but because you are deserving of it. By shifting from doing to receiving, you can step into the life you have always dreamed of and you'll find that life often offers you even more than you imagined.

This is not about passivity, it is about openness. It's about trusting the journey you have been on and allowing yourself to embrace what is already on its way to you. It is about acknowledging that your work has been significant, and now, the universe is ready to meet you by bringing the opportunities, love, and abundance you have long been seeking. What you are seeking is seeking you.

So now, as you continue your journey, know that you are ready. You have laid the foundation, and the life you desire is already here waiting for you to receive it with open arms and a trusting heart.

## The Practice of Receiving: How to Open Yourself to the Life You Deserve

1. **Acknowledge the Work You've Done.** Take a moment to reflect on all the work you've already done. Look at the growth you've experienced, the healing you've accomplished, and the strength you've discovered within yourself. This is not a small feat. It is a profound transformation, and you deserve to celebrate every single step. You don't have to wait until you've reached the end of a journey to feel proud. Honor the progress you've made and acknowledge that you are already worthy of everything you desire.

2. **Release the Need to Prove Yourself.** It's time to let go of the belief that you must prove your worthiness. Stop measuring your value based on your output or your ability to meet external standards. Your worth is inherent in your being, not in your

doing. You don't have to constantly prove yourself to others or even to yourself. Trust that you are enough, exactly as you are. By releasing the pressure to perform, you free yourself to receive the gifts that life has in store for you.

3. **Practice Gratitude for What's Already Here.** Gratitude is a powerful tool for opening up to abundance. By focusing on what you already have, you shift your energy from a place of lack to one of abundance. Take time each day to express gratitude for the things that are already in your life, your health, your relationships, your creativity, your growth. This practice helps you recognize that you are already living a life that is worthy of your dreams. The more you focus on the blessings you have, the more room you create for new blessings to flow into your life.

4. **Be Open to Receiving.** It's easy to block yourself from receiving when you don't feel worthy or when you've been conditioned to think that you must work for everything. But receiving is just as much a part of the process as giving. Begin to open yourself to receiving love, support, opportunities, and abundance. Say yes to the things that are aligned with your heart's desires. Let yourself experience joy, relaxation, and pleasure without guilt. Trust that you are deserving of the life you are creating.

5. **Visualize the Life You Want to Receive.** Take time each day to visualize the life you want to receive. Imagine it in full detail what does your life look like, feel like, taste like? Picture yourself living in this life with ease, joy, and peace. Don't just imagine your physical accomplishments; focus on the emotional and spiritual experience of receiving your dreams. Allow yourself to feel the gratitude and excitement that comes with the knowledge that this life is already yours to receive.

## The Life You Imagine and More

The truth is that the life you have been imagining for yourself is likely just the beginning. When you open yourself to receiving the gifts of the universe, you'll discover that the life you receive may exceed what you could have ever imagined. You may find that opportunities, relationships, and experiences flow to you in ways that surprise and delight you.

You are deserving of all the peace, joy, abundance, and love the world offers. You have done the work. Now, trust that the universe is aligning with you, and you are worthy of receiving everything that comes your way.

You are not meant to chase or force life into being. You are meant to receive it, to allow it to unfold naturally, and to trust that you are in the perfect place to receive the blessings that await you.

So, take a deep breath, dear one. Receive the life you've been dreaming of your heart's desire. Then, receive a life that is even more than you ever imagined.

## Meet Tiffany

Tiffany is a 42-year-old creative strategist who had spent most of her adult life feeling emotionally exiled in professional and personal circles. Exceptionally intuitive and gifted from a young age, she learned early on that her depth made others uncomfortable. In meetings, her insights were often met with blank stares or deflected with humor. In friendships, she found herself becoming the confidante, rarely the one confiding. A neurodivergent woman with a gifted mind and a heart that felt deeply, she had learned to outwork, outthink, and outperform everyone around her. Her calendar was always full, her accomplishments impressive, her energy stretched to its edge. She was the person others called strong. Driven. Inspiring.

Under all that output lived a growing exhaustion. The harder Tiffany worked, the more disconnected she felt from joy, from purpose, from herself. She kept reaching for success as if it were a finish line, believing that once she got *there*, the peace she longed for would finally arrive. But each milestone came with the same hollow whisper: *Now what?*

Everything began to shift during a sabbatical she hadn't planned an unexpected health scare forced her to stop. With no projects to manage and no deadlines to chase, Tiffany was left alone with herself. And for the first time in years, she listened.

She began journaling, walking without a destination, and re-reading the notes from her earlier therapy sessions. Patterns emerged: the deep belief that she had to earn love, that stillness was laziness, that receiving was selfish. These stories weren't hers, they were inherited, reinforced, and absorbed over time.

She began to ask: What if I'm already enough? What if receiving is actually wisdom in action?

Bit by bit, Tiffany experimented with doing less and allowing more. She practiced gratitude, not as a checkbox, but as a felt experience. She visualized the life she truly wanted, not the life that looked impressive, but the one that felt nourishing. She noticed how the right opportunities began to flow not through hustle, but through alignment.

Today, Tiffany lives and works differently. She still leads, still creates from a place of being grounded, not urgency. She surrounds herself with people who support her without requiring performance. She trusts her pace. Above all, she allows herself to receive rest, love, abundance, joy. Not as a reward for exhaustion, but as her birthright.

## Reflection Questions

1. Where in your life have you been striving to prove your worth through doing or achieving? (Bring awareness to patterns of exerting too much effort or seeking validation through output.)

2. What beliefs about worthiness or success have you inherited that no longer serve you? (Consider messages from family, school, or society that you've internalized.)

3. What might it feel like to live from a place of receiving rather than chasing? (Visualize what spaciousness, receptivity, and ease could look like for you.)

4. How can you begin to honor the work you've already done without needing to do more? (This may include rituals of acknowledgment, celebration, or simple stillness.)

5. What small act of receiving can you welcome into your life this week? (Think of something that allows you to soften, receive support, or embrace joy.)

## PART 7

# NAVIGATING RELATIONSHIPS

# CHAPTER 46

# LONELINESS AND THE SEARCH FOR KINDRED SPIRITS

Loneliness is the absence of resonance. It is the hollow space left when no one mirrors your inner world. For the neurodivergent soul, gifted, intuitive, sensitive, this isn't a rare occurrence. It's a recurring ache, often woven into the fabric of everyday life. You can stand in a crowded room, engage in polite conversation, meet social expectations and still feel like your essence is floating just out of reach from others' perception.

This is not about a lack of company. It's the disconnection that happens when your depth has no place to land. Surface-level interactions drain rather than energize. Pretending to be "fine" becomes a default mask, worn so frequently it almost feels like a second skin. Yet beneath it, a quiet desperation grows the need to be known as you are, without dilution.

For gifted adults, conversation that skims the surface often feels like static. Words without substance feel like noise. There is a hunger for substance, for truth spoken in real time, for connection that doesn't require you to shrink or stretch to fit someone else's frame. You don't seek more relationships, you seek *right* relationships. The kind that stirs your inner compass. The kind where energy speaks before words arrive.

Loneliness, in this context, is not a symptom. It is a signal. It points toward the hunger for authenticity, the desire to exhale in someone's presence without fear of misinterpretation. The neurodivergent soul craves connection that doesn't come with a translation cost. We want shared frequency, not performance.

This is why forced socializing often increases the ache. More noise, more masks, more of what doesn't fit. What soothes is resonance. That moment when someone's presence feels like a homecoming. That moment when silence between two people holds more truth than hours of talking ever could.

Kindred spirits are not found through formulas or checklists. They are recognized through the quiet knowing that says, you don't need to hide here. These connections do not demand you prove, explain, or edit yourself. They hold space. They witness. They reflect you back to yourself with clarity and care.

To find these souls, you must first honor your own. Learn the shape of your own truth. Grieve the places where connection failed you. Name your longings without apology. Build a life where your inner world has room to breathe, even before others enter it.

Not every interaction will offer resonance. Not every person will understand your language. That's not a failure, it's a filter. It clears the way for those rare, radiant connections that don't just accompany you, but *meet* you.

Kindred spirits exist. They are not imaginary or out of reach. They are out there, moving through the world with the same ache and the same hope. When you live in alignment with your truth, you become easier to find. When two resonant souls meet, even briefly, loneliness loses its grip.

### Meet Paul

Paul is a 41-year-old gifted creative strategist who has built a successful career helping companies innovate. On paper, he had it all, clients, accolades, a downtown loft. But inside, he was profoundly lonely. He described feeling like a "perpetual alien" deeply aware, emotionally intense, and always out of sync.

Despite being in frequent contact with colleagues and collaborators, Paul rarely felt a sense of true connection. He could play the part, deliver the pitch, and even enjoy small talk at times. But he often left social events feeling drained and disoriented. "It's like I can hear the music playing," he said, "but I'm not dancing to the same rhythm as everyone else."

Therapy helped Paul recognize his lifelong pattern of masking, hiding his depth to fit into social spaces that felt emotionally shallow. He was exhausted from playing roles that earned approval but cost him authenticity.

After naming his loneliness, Paul committed to seeking out resonance rather than performance. He joined a small online forum for gifted adults and began having conversations that felt nourishing instead of numbing. Through shared language and unspoken understanding, he met two others with whom he formed a consistent, safe circle of connection.

It wasn't about quantity; it was about soul-level quality. Paul's relationships began to shift, too; by being more himself, he magnetized others who could meet him where he truly lived.

"Loneliness didn't leave overnight," he reflected. "But when I stopped performing and started trusting my inner rhythm, the kindred spirits began to find me."

Loneliness is not just a feeling, it's a signal. It calls us toward a deeper knowing of ourselves and a deeper commitment to seek out those who speak our soul's language. In the next chapter, we'll explore how sensitivity and intuition act as internal compasses, guiding neurodivergent individuals toward the people, environments, and rhythms that restore and revive. These inner gifts, when honored, become the very tools that help us find our place in a world that too often asks us to hide.

## Reflection Questions

1. How do you currently experience loneliness? Is it situational, chronic, or somewhere in between?

2. What does "resonance" mean to you in relationships? Can you recall a moment when you felt seen without having to explain yourself?

3. In what ways have you masked or minimized your neurodivergent traits to fit in socially?

4. Are there environments, online or offline, where you feel more like your true self? What might happen if you gave those spaces more time or energy?

5. Who in your life brings out your natural rhythm? Are there people you feel "lighter" with? What would it mean to prioritize those connections?

# CHAPTER 47

# BOUNDARIES FOR THE HYPER-EMPATHIC SOUL

Neurodivergent people often develop a profound capacity for empathy from an early age. We know when something is wrong, even if it is never spoken aloud. We feel the distress of others, absorb the tension, and intuit the undertones. In relationships, we are often the emotional "thermometers," picking up what others miss or deny.

With this depth comes vulnerability. Without adequate emotional scaffolding, boundaries, co-regulation, and recovery time empathy turns into emotional flooding. The world's pain becomes your own. Your nervous system remains in a heightened state, overstimulated not just by sound or light, but by feeling itself.

Add to this the common experience of emotional invalidation being told "you're too sensitive," "you're overreacting," or "you take things too personally" and what was once a natural gift becomes a source of shame. Many neurodivergent individuals learn to shut down, numb out, or disconnect from their emotional wisdom just to survive.

**Communicating Your Needs Without Apologizing**

For many neurodivergent souls, expressing needs can feel like walking a tightrope between authenticity and alienation. The fear isn't just that our needs won't be met, but that they'll be judged, dismissed, or misunderstood. From an early age, many of us internalize the message that our differences make us "difficult," "too sensitive," "too much," or "not enough." Over time, these messages morph into apologies. Not just for our needs, but for our very being.

Apologies become armor. We preface requests with "I'm sorry," soften our truths to protect others from discomfort, and downplay our boundaries to avoid being labeled selfish or dramatic. While meant to ease communication, these habits often erode self-worth. They teach us to filter our authenticity through the lens of someone else's comfort.

But what if the act of asking is not an inconvenience, but a form of sacred self-respect?

Unapologetically communicating your needs clearly, directly, and is a powerful reclamation of your right to fully exist. It affirms that your sensory, emotional, and cognitive landscapes are not defects to be hidden, but vital aspects of your humanity to be honored.

This doesn't mean being harsh or indifferent to others, it means being aligned. When you express a need without apology, you are not demanding; you are inviting. You are creating a bridge one built not on shame, but on clarity, consent, and care.

**From Apology to Affirmation**

When you shift from saying: "I'm sorry, but I can't do that," to "That doesn't work for me right now," You're not closing a door; you're opening one to a more honest interaction.

When you say: "I need some quiet time to recharge," instead of "Sorry I'm being antisocial," You invite others to understand you instead of misunderstanding you.

This shift is subtle but transformative. It requires self-awareness, emotional regulation, and sometimes a lot of courage. But the payoff is immense: more aligned relationships, a deeper sense of self-trust, and a life where your nervous system is not constantly performing for approval.

**Practical Tips to Communicate Without Apologizing**

1. **Notice Your Language**: Pay attention to how often you say

"sorry" when expressing a need. Is it really an apology or just a placeholder for discomfort?
2. **Practice Reframing**: Instead of "Sorry I need a break," try "I'm going to take a short break so I can come back grounded."
3. **Validate Internally First**: Remind yourself, *"My needs are valid, even if they're different from others'."* Start by giving yourself the permission you're seeking externally.
4. **Use "I" Statements**: Express needs from your own experience. "I need..." or "I feel more supported when..." reduces defensiveness and keeps the focus on your reality.
5. **Build a Support Vocabulary**: Practice phrases like "This supports me best," "This helps me feel safe," or "This is what I need to participate fully."

## Reclaiming Your Voice

When you speak your needs with grounded clarity, not in apology but in truth, you take up rightful space in the world. You stop shrinking to fit into others' expectations and instead begin sculpting a life that fits you.

This isn't about perfection or never feeling anxious. It's about showing up with the courage to name what matters, even when your voice shakes. Over time, your voice steadies. Your confidence grows. And so does your capacity to be both fully yourself and fully connected.

Communicating your needs without apology is a courageous and empowering step toward self-respect and authentic living. It challenges the old scripts of shame and invites you to stand firmly in your truth with compassion for yourself and for those around you.

Remember, clear communication not only honors your neurodivergent soul but also creates space for genuine connection and mutual understanding. Your needs are valid, your voice is worthy, and you deserve to be heard exactly as you are.

As you grow more confident in expressing your needs clearly and without apology, you begin to build the foundation for deeper, more authentic relationships. This clarity not only helps others understand you better but also guides you toward finding spaces and people who truly see and support your neurodivergent soul. Connection is a vital element of care, and the next chapter explores how to find or create a community where your unique rhythms, perspectives, and gifts are not just accepted but celebrated.

## Meet Gene

Gene is a 42-year-old man who says he has ADHD and autism who has spent years feeling invisible in both personal and professional relationships. Early on, he learned that his need for quiet spaces or extra time to process information was often dismissed or met with impatience. Over time, Gene internalized a belief that asking for accommodations was "asking too much," leading him to apologize excessively whenever he voiced his needs.

In our mentoring sessions, Gene began to recognize how this pattern undermined his confidence and strained his relationships.

Together, we worked on practical strategies:

- **Reframing needs as natural and valid:** Gene practiced stating his needs as facts rather than excuses. For example, "I work best with fewer distractions," rather than "I'm sorry to be difficult, but I need quiet."
- **Using clear, calm language:** He learned to communicate directly and kindly, which helped others understand rather than feel defensive.
- **Building a script for common scenarios:** Gene prepared phrases to express his boundaries or requests in a way that felt authentic and respectful.
- **Practicing self-compassion:** When old feelings of guilt or shame arose, Gene reminded himself that needing support is part of being human, not a fault.

Over time, Gene noticed a shift. People began responding with more respect and cooperation, and he felt lighter and more empowered. He no longer saw his needs as burdens, but as essential parts of his well-being deserving of care.

**Reflection Questions**

1. In what situations do I most often feel compelled to apologize for my needs? Why?

2. What message have I internalized about being "too much" or "too different"? How has that message shaped how I express myself today?

3. What would it feel like to state a need without softening it or apologizing for it? Can I imagine that moment?

4. How might honoring my needs more clearly shift my relationships with others and with myself?

5. What is one specific boundary or request I want to express this week without apology? What words will I use?

CHAPTER 48

# FINDING YOUR NEURODIVERGENT COMMUNITY

Living as a neurodivergent soul can often feel like navigating a beautiful but unmarked path through a world designed for others. The terrain may be unfamiliar, and the travelers are few and far between. Many gifted, autistic, ADHD, or otherwise neurodivergent individuals know the ache of feeling like the "only one" who sees, feels, or processes things differently. Yet at the heart of every neurodivergent soul lies a longing not just to be accepted, but to be *heard, loved, and understood.*

Finding your neurodivergent community is not just about meeting others who share diagnostic labels, it's about finding a space where your unique way of being is welcomed without caveat. Where your tangents are followed, your sensitivities respected, your passions celebrated. A space where you don't have to explain the "why" behind your needs. You simply *are*, and that is enough.

**Community as Sanctuary and Mirror**
True community becomes a sanctuary. It is a gentle mirror that reflects your wholeness, especially in moments when the world tells you that you're fragmented or flawed. It is where deep laughter lives, where inside jokes born from shared struggles and strange gifts become healing in themselves. It's where others can remind you

(even on days when you forget) that your wiring is brilliantly different. The others can reflect to you your light, reminding you who you are just as you are for them.

Your neurodivergent community can take many forms:
- Creative or maker spaces where authenticity thrives
- Online forums with thoughtful moderation
- Quiet, low-stimulation gatherings that honor sensory needs
- Faith-based or spiritual circles that allow room for depth and nuance
- Peer-led support groups centered on ADHD, autism, giftedness, or twice-exceptionality
- Close friendships built slowly, intentionally, and with mutual care
- Craft or creative groups like writing, quilting, sewing, wood working, etc.

It may also include mentorships, therapeutic spaces, or intergenerational connections that foster wisdom-sharing. These relationships, whether occasional or daily, can become soul-nourishing connections that remind you that belonging is more about finding your people than about fitting into a group that is not meant for you.

### The Power of Multiple Peer Groups
No single person or group will meet all your social, intellectual, emotional, and creative needs and that's okay. In fact, embracing multiple peer groups can be an empowering strategy for feeling fully supported and expressed.

One circle may be where your intellectual intensity is met and matched, while another allows space for emotional sensitivity and processing. You might have a small online group for special interests, a weekly creative cohort, a trusted group of neurodivergent professionals, and a nature-based friend or two who understands your need for solitude and spaciousness.

There is freedom in not expecting one person or group to be your everything. When you allow yourself to belong in multiple places for different reasons, your social landscape becomes less about scarcity and more about abundance. You can move between groups based on your current energy, bandwidth, and need for depth, play, activism, or rest.

And you may find that some connections are seasonal or situational and that, too, is part of the rhythm of authentic relating.

## Trusting the Process

Finding or creating a sense of community often takes time, especially if you've been hurt, excluded, or misunderstood in the past. It's okay to feel cautious. Your nervous system may need gentle pacing, slow trust-building, and clear boundaries. Not every space will be safe or supportive and part of your empowerment is in saying *no* to what doesn't feel aligned.

Community is about cultivating resonant relationships rather than collecting people. Listen for that hum of recognition when you meet someone who *gets you*. That feeling of being seen, without having to explain your entire life, is powerful and can feel electric and awe inspired. The people who get you are your people. Let them in at a pace that is comfortable for you. Moving too fast or too slow can add unanticipated challenges. Take the time to tend to your relationships with care.

Know that if you haven't yet found them, you're not behind. You're simply in the in-between a sacred space of becoming.

## Meet Elena

Elena is a 35-year-old woman author who has spent years feeling profoundly alone in her neurodivergence. She had tried joining various online forums and local groups, only to find that many spaces either lacked true understanding or were dominated by voices that didn't resonate with her.

After working with me, Elena realized she needed to shift her approach. Instead of searching for a "perfect" community, she began creating one. She started a small writing group for neurodivergent creatives in her city, emphasizing openness, acceptance, and shared vulnerability.

This community became a lifeline. Within this circle, Elena found encouragement for her creative work, compassionate listeners for her struggles, and a safe place to explore her identity without apology.

Over time, the group grew organically and became a vibrant hub of connection and healing. Elena's story reminds us that sometimes, finding your community means becoming a community-builder, a courageous act that honors both yourself and others.

Finding your neurodivergent community is a vital act of self-care, a way to move from isolation toward connection, from survival toward belonging. As you build or discover your village, you cultivate a network of support that nurtures your soul and celebrates your unique gifts.

Finding your neurodivergent community is more than locating others like you. It is discovering a space where your soul feels recognized, your struggles understood, and your strengths celebrated. In this shared belonging, you find not only support but also empowerment to live fully and authentically. Remember, building or joining your community is a journey of gentle courage, one that nourishes your spirit and reminds you that you are never truly alone.

## Reflection Questions

1. What does a nourishing community feel like for you on a sensory, emotional, and spiritual level?

2. Where in your life do you currently feel most seen or understood? Where do you feel the most pressure to mask?

3. What would it look like to build or find multiple peer groups that support different aspects of who you are?

4. What past experiences, positive or painful, have shaped your current approach to connection?

5. How can you begin inviting more belonging into your life in small, sustainable ways this week?

## CHAPTER 49

# LOVE IN TRANSLATION – INTIMACY WITH A DIFFERENT OPERATING SYSTEM

To be neurodivergent in a relationship, whether romantic, platonic, or familial, is to live in a world where connection often collides with misinterpretation. Love, for many neurodivergent souls, doesn't lack presence or power; it simply moves through channels that are often unseen or misread by others. We love with a depth that can be oceanic, a sincerity that is sometimes startling, and a devotion that may not follow conventional scripts. But when our way of showing care doesn't align with neurotypical expectations, it can feel like trying to sync two systems running entirely different code.

It's not that we lack the capacity for intimacy far from it. We often long for closeness, but we approach it on our own terms: through passion-fueled monologues, shared silence, carefully crafted rituals, or meticulous acts of service. Our version of intimacy might be sending a partner dozens of articles about their favorite subject, quietly remembering the smallest details they mention, or coexisting in quiet parallel play. What looks distant from the outside can be sacred from the inside.

### When Two Neurodivergent People Love

When two neurodivergent individuals come together, there is often a kind of shorthand, a natural understanding that certain things don't need to be explained or justified. Eye contact isn't forced. Silence isn't awkward. Boundaries are honored instinctively. The social performance is dialed down, and in its place comes a beautiful authenticity.

But even within this shared neurodivergence, differences arise. One person may stim to self-sooth, while the other may need stillness to feel regulated. One may hyperfocus on tasks and forget to eat, while the other needs routine and structure to feel safe. One might communicate love through logic and analysis, the other through creative storytelling or sensory expression. These contrasts require conscious tending.

In these partnerships, emotional labor can be a shared endeavor rather than a one-sided strain. There can be a mutual commitment to developing shared language to defining terms, creating cues, and respecting downtime. Misunderstandings still happen, but there's often more grace extended, more room for "I need a moment" and "Can we try that again?" There is space for love to be messy and nonlinear.

True resonance in these relationships comes not from sameness, but from mutual validation: You are not too much. I see how you love. And I love you, too in my way.

### When a Neurodivergent and a Neurotypical Person Love

In relationships between a neurodivergent and a neurotypical partner, the potential for growth and challenge is especially profound. These pairings often confront the limits of unspoken norms. The neurotypical partner may expect certain behaviors as indicators of affection spontaneous compliments, eye contact, predictable expressions of empathy while the neurodivergent partner may be expressing love in subtler, less traditional ways. Without conscious awareness, both can begin to feel unseen and misunderstood.

The neurotypical person might interpret a need for solitude as disinterest. The neurodivergent person might feel overwhelmed by constant conversation or physical affection. What begins as confusion can deepen into resentment unless both commit to a deeper understanding of each other's internal world.

This dynamic calls for radical curiosity, not just tolerance. The neurotypical partner must learn to interpret different expressions of love without pathologizing them. The neurodivergent partner must learn to communicate their needs without shame or apology. Both must dismantle assumptions that there is only one correct way to love or be loved.

It helps when both people ask questions like:
- *What does safety feel like to you?*
- *How do you know when someone cares?*
- *What makes you feel overwhelmed?*
- *What's something you wish I'd notice more often?*

By slowing down and moving away from default settings, these relationships can become transformative. They often require more conscious work, but they also yield deeper insight, compassion, and intimacy. They invite both partners to love each other not *despite* their differences, but *through* them.

## Building the Bridge

For any neurodivergent person, whether partnered with someone neurodivergent or neurotypical intimacy is a language that must be learned, not assumed. It is rarely automatic. It requires naming things most people leave unsaid. It requires scaffolding: a shared framework of agreements, signals, and emotional lexicons that help both partners navigate each other's internal landscapes.

This process is not about "fixing" or "normalizing" anyone. It's about meeting one another with honesty and care. It's about co-authoring a love story that defies the standard template and instead asks, "What do we need to feel known, safe, and cherished"?

The goal isn't to erase the operating system differences, but to honor them. To become translators for one another, not editors. To say, "Your language of love may not be mine, but I will learn it because I care enough to listen differently."

True intimacy, especially across neurotypes, isn't built on effortless chemistry. It's built on the bravery to be seen, the patience to learn, and the devotion to hold space for someone's full, unfiltered self. In that space, love becomes more than communication. It becomes communion.

## Meet Alex and Jordan

Alex (gifted and autistic) and Jordan (neurotypical) had been together for four years and often described their relationship as "beautifully confusing." Alex expressed love through carefully thought-out acts, preparing Jordan's favorite coffee blend, researching solutions to their partner's work stress, and building routines that kept their shared life calm. Jordan, on the other hand, loved spontaneity, emotional expressiveness, and verbal affection.

At first, they clashed often. Jordan felt unloved because Alex didn't say "I love you" very often or initiate cuddles. Alex felt overwhelmed by Jordan's frequent need for verbal reassurance and interpreted it as distrust. The turning point came when they engaged in couples mentoring that honored neurodiversity, inspired by principles from my mentoring work that emphasize translation, not transformation.

Through structured conversations and journaling practices, they created a "love lexicon", a shared understanding of each other's cues and needs. Alex began using sticky notes to express emotions, a method that felt authentic but manageable. Jordan learned to recognize Alex's acts of service as genuine intimacy. Over time, their love deepened not by changing who they were, but by honoring each other's native languages. They now describe their relationship as "a daily dance of translation and trust."

As we learn to honor intimacy across different operating systems, we also begin to see the value of emotional self-trust. Navigating relationships as a neurodivergent soul requires more than external understanding, it calls for an inner anchoring in our own truth. In the next chapter, *Rebuilding Trust with Your Own Nervous System*, we turn inward to explore how reclaiming that trust can transform both how we love and how we live.

## Reflection Questions

1. In what ways do you naturally express love or care that may not fit typical expectations? Consider both verbal and nonverbal expressions, your routines, habits, gifts, or actions that are your personal language of love.

2. When have you felt most deeply understood in a relationship? What helped that connection feel safe, and how might you recreate or advocate for that kind of understanding now?

3. What misunderstandings about your way of connecting have caused you pain or self-doubt? How can you begin to release internalized shame around those differences?

4. What are your needs around emotional safety, sensory comfort, and communication in intimate relationships? Have you clearly named those needs for yourself and are you able to share them with others?

5. How might you begin or continue building a shared "translation guide" with someone important in your life? Think about one specific dynamic (past or present) where mutual curiosity and clearer language could shift the connection.

# CHAPTER 50

# SAFETY IN NEURODIVERGENT RELATIONSHIPS

Every meaningful relationship begins with one essential element: safety. Safety within any relationship indicates the presence of alignment. For your neurodivergent soul, this kind of safety cannot exist without a foundational trust in your own nervous system.

Safety encompasses emotional safety, physical safety, mental safety, sexual safety and spiritual safety at the core. Emotional safety is when you are free to share your feelings without fear of ridicule or harm such as gaslighting or being demeaned. Physical safety is present when you are safe physically and you can relax, knowing that you are not in danger. Mental safety is present when you can share your ideas, thoughts and beliefs without trepidation. Sexual safety is when you can express your authentic identity without the fear of being rejected or harmed in some way. All of these are essential in close relationships.

Sadly, many people were raised without these levels of safety present in a consistent manner. This impacts on your ability to engage in a healthy, safe relationship as an adult until you do your inner work to heal the old wounds. It takes work to establish and maintain a healthy relationship.

In relationships, especially intimate ones, many neurodivergent individuals have learned to override their internal cues in order to preserve connection. We've pushed through sensory overload to be present, said "yes" when our bodies screamed "no," masked emotional needs to avoid being called "too much." Over time, this compromises our ability to know when we're actually safe or when we're not. Without that internal clarity, trust in ourselves and others begins to fracture.

The body keeps the score and it also holds the wisdom. Rebuilding trust with your nervous system is about learning to listen to the subtle (and sometimes loud) signals it gives you, especially in relational settings. Does your chest tighten around certain people? Do you feel unexpectedly exhausted after a conversation? Does your stomach clench even when someone says they "mean well"? These are not inconveniences to be ignored. They are information. And for the neurodivergent soul, learning to trust these cues is a sacred part of relational healing.

In many traditional relationships, compromise is taught as the path to harmony. But for neurodivergent individuals, compromise without body-honoring awareness can lead to self-erasure. We need somatic consent more than conflict resolution. We need to know when we are still present in ourselves while connecting with another. The moment we begin to leave ourselves behind for the sake of someone else's comfort, the relationship becomes unsafe, even if unintentionally.

To rebuild your nervous system trust in a relational context means:
- Slowing down interactions enough to feel your body's "yes" or "no."
- Noticing when a conversation begins to feel overstimulating or overwhelming.
- Giving yourself permission to pause, to breathe, to walk away without shame.
- Letting yourself speak up when something feels off, even if you're not sure why.

When you begin honoring your nervous system in relationships, you teach others how to honor it too. You set a precedent that connection must include your full presence, not just a curated or contorted version of yourself.

And as trust in your own signals grows, so does the clarity of who is truly safe for you. You begin to distinguish between relationships that nourish you and those that require you to constantly self-abandon. That discernment is a form of liberation.

## Radical Intimacy Emerges from Self-Love

For many neurodivergent souls, intimacy has long felt like a risky performance. We've been trained to filter ourselves to speak, behave, and even feel in ways that make others more comfortable. We've learned which parts of us are "too much" or "too different" and tried to edit ourselves into something more palatable. In the process, we have often sacrificed our truth at the altar of belonging. True intimacy cannot thrive behind a mask.

Unmasking is a sacred act of self-love rather than disclosure for the sake of explanation. It is saying to yourself, "I am worthy of being seen as I am, not as who others expect me to be." It is understood that hiding, even when it protects you, can slowly erode your soul. When you choose to unmask from a place of self-honoring rather than survival, you open the door to radical intimacy, the kind of connection that is welcomed, not earned. Radical intimacy does not require perfection. It requires presence.

When you love yourself enough to stop managing how others perceive you, the way you show up in relationships transforms. You stop bending yourself into shapes that hurt. You stop tolerating connections that require self-erasure. You start letting yourself be known. And in that knowing, something sacred emerges relationships built on mutual revelation, not performance.

Clearly, unmasking is vulnerable work. It may bring up grief for the years spent hiding. It may invite discomfort as others adjust or fail to adjust. It may mean some relationships fall away. But what remains is honest. And what grows from that honesty is a connection rooted in truth.

Self-love is not a precondition you must master before being in a relationship. It is the soil in which intimacy takes root. When you treat yourself with reverence, others learn to do the same. And when they don't, your body and your heart will know.

Radical intimacy begins inside. It is not about being more available to others. It is about being fully available to yourself.

**Meet Rena**

Rena is a woman who has late-diagnosed autism in her 40s who has spent most of her adult life shapeshifting in relationships. She could read social cues expertly, mimic others' rhythms, and intuit what they needed, skills that kept her relationships smooth on the surface but left her exhausted and unseen. "Everyone thought I was easy to be with," she said, "but I didn't feel like *me* in any of it."

After years of burnout and a painful divorce, Rena began working with me in a mentoring process focused on self-recognition. She wrote letters to her younger self, practiced mirror work, and slowly dismantled the belief that being loved required being less of herself.

She began unmasking in small but powerful ways of telling a friend she needed text instead of phone calls, allowing herself to stim in front of her new partner, wearing noise-canceling headphones on dates. Each act reinforced the truth: *I am allowed to exist as I am.*

Over time, Rena's relationship with herself softened. The inner critic gave way to an inner companion. Her relationships, once built on performance, became spacious and real. She told me, "The more I show up as me, the more love I actually feel. Not because people changed, but because I stopped hiding."

**Reflection Questions**

1. What bodily cues arise for you when you feel safe or unsafe in a relationship?

2. In what ways have you overridden your own signals and inner knowing to maintain a sense of connection?

3. What would it feel like to pause a conversation or interaction to check in with your body?

4. Are there any current relationships where your nervous system feels consistently dysregulated? What is your body trying to tell you?

5. How might you begin honoring your nervous system more fully without guilt or apology?

CONCLUSION

# COMING HOME TO YOURSELF

If you've made it to this final page, I want to thank you for allowing yourself to be seen. *Care for the Neurodivergent Soul* is more than a book; it's an inspired revolution coming in quiet confidence. It is a reclaiming and a deep breath in a world that often feels like it's often harsh while moving too fast for the beautifully complex ways we experience life.

Throughout these pages, I've invited you into the tender, often-unspoken realities of being gifted, neurodivergent or otherwise different by design. We've explored cycles of energy and shutdown, the ache of loneliness, the nuances of intimacy, and the radical act of rest. We've named truths that are too often buried beneath shame, survival, or sheer exhaustion.

And yet, this is not the end. It's the beginning. Your beginning of a profound reawakening of your innermost authenticity that is begging to emerge into the world! Come out and play with me.

The path forward is not one-size-fits-all. It is as unique as your inner compass. My hope is that the reflections, stories, and practices in this book have helped you remember what you've always known deep down: You are not broken. You are brilliantly designed for a different kind of life with rich, vibrant experiences as well as profound awakenings. Awakenings that can often feel messy and brilliant at the same time.

As you integrate what resonates, I invite you to keep going gently and with curiosity, compassion, and sacred reverence for your inner world. Leave behind or share with another what may not be for you at this time.

If you feel called to connect more deeply, you are welcome in my space. I offer one-on-one Get to Know You Calls, mentoring for gifted professionals, and live community conversations where we continue to explore what it means to thrive with a different operating system. You can learn more at VisionsApplied.com or MsDianneAllen.com or find me on Instagram and Facebook @dianne_a_allen

You are not alone, and you never have been, even when it felt like it at times.

Thank you for bringing your whole self to these pages. I see you. I honor and respect you. I am cheering you on as you continue to care for your beautifully neurodivergent soul.

With all my heart,

Dianne A. Allen, MA

## Acknowledgments

This book would not exist without the many soul level connections that have shaped and supported my journey both personally and professionally. Each page is woven with lived experience, lifelong education, deep listening, and the stories of gifted and neurodivergent souls who have trusted me with their truth.

I offer my heartfelt gratitude to Michelle Royal, whose dedication letter so beautifully captures the essence of my work. Michelle's unwavering belief in my vision and her intuitive gift for language inspired the very title of this book. Her friendship and insight have been a steady beacon through seasons of both clarity and confusion.

A special thank you to Sara Julian, whose foreword brings depth, resonance, and grounding to the start of this book. Her wisdom, vulnerability, and powerful articulation of the neurodivergent experience reflect a kind, courageous presence that is important in this world. Her words offer a mirror to every reader seeking belonging.

To Nic Albright, thank you for your creative brilliance, steady support, and the countless ways you helped shape the visual and energetic expression of this work. Your artistry and care are felt in more ways than one.

To Abbie Jones, your consistent presence, encouragement, and behind-the-scenes support have made such a meaningful difference. I am deeply grateful for the way you show up, again and again, with grace and heart.

To the brilliant, sensitive, often overwhelmed gifted and neurodivergent individuals I have had the honor of mentoring: your courage to keep showing up to feel, to question, and to reclaim yourselves is what lights the way. This book is for you and because of you.

To my own inner younger self, who felt "too much" and "not

enough" all at once, thank you for staying curious, even when the world didn't make space for your truth. You are safe now.

And to the many unnamed teachers, clients, colleagues, and kindred spirits who have shared their wisdom along the way, your fingerprints are on these pages too!

With all my gratitude and deep respect,

*Dianne A. Allen, MA*

# Love Letters to Your Neurodivergent Soul

This section is a gentle offering, a soft space where compassion meets truth. These love letters are written for your heart that have often felt like too much, not enough, or alone and misunderstood.

These love letters are for the minds that move differently and beautifully. For the souls who have been told implicitly or directly that their way of being is inconvenient, overwhelming, or wrong.

Here, you will find reminders stitched with tenderness and strength:

You are not too much.
You are worthy of care.
You belong here.
You are not alone.

Each letter is a mirror, reflecting to you the dignity and inherent worth of your neurodivergent existence. Whether you are autistic, ADHD, intensely sensitive, or identify in any way outside the neurotypical mold, these words are for you. Let the words meet you where you are and remind you: you belong.

## You Are Not Too Much

Dear One,

I see you. I see your beautiful, intricate, and ever-evolving soul. I see the way your mind dances with endless ideas, the way your heart beats with uncontainable empathy, and the way your spirit moves through the world, sometimes quietly and sometimes with intensity. I see how deeply you feel and how fiercely you care. You are not invisible to me. I want you to know that with every fiber of your being that you are not too much.

I know the world has sometimes told you that you are. Maybe it has made you feel that your sensitivity is overwhelming, your energy is exhausting, or your thoughts are too vast for the ordinary spaces around you. Perhaps you've been made to feel that your emotions, your pace, your ways of thinking everything that makes you, you are simply too much for the world to bear.

I want to tell you, from the deepest place of truth I can offer, you are not too much. You are exactly enough. You are not meant to fit into a world that demands uniformity. You are a soul meant to stand out, to bring new ideas, to challenge the norms, to heal in ways others may never understand. Your sensitivity is a gift, not a flaw. Your depth is a blessing. The way you feel so deeply, the way you experience life in full color, is what makes you powerful, beautiful, and irreplaceable.

There is nothing wrong with the way you experience the world. There is nothing too much about the way your mind works, the way you process the world with such exquisite attention to detail, the way you care about others so deeply. You are a wellspring of creativity, emotion, insight, and love. Your very presence is a light in a world that too often forgets to notice what matters most.

It's okay if you don't always fit in. It's okay if your pace is different, if your needs are different, if your way of expressing yourself is different. The world needs what you have to offer, even if it sometimes forgets to make room for it. You were not meant to shrink yourself or fit into the tiny box that others may have tried to put you in. You were meant to stretch the edges of possibility, to challenge and inspire, to show others what it means to be truly alive in all of your complexity.

You are not too much. Your brilliance does not need to be dimmed to make others more comfortable. Your energy does not need to be suppressed because the world cannot keep up. You are not too much for the space you occupy, and you never will be. Your heart is a well of compassion, your mind a source of limitless potential. You have everything within you to live the life that feels true.

On the days when the world feels too loud, too demanding, too unforgiving, remember that you are allowed to rest. You are allowed to take a step back and give yourself the space to recharge. Your worth is not measured by your productivity or how well you fit into the world's narrow ideas of success. You are worthy simply because you exist. You bring a unique and irreplaceable light to this world. You are perfect, just as you are. I see you!

With all my love and deepest admiration,

*Dianne*

## You Are Worthy of Care

Dear One,

I want to begin by telling you something so deeply important, so fundamental to your existence that I hope you hear it in the very marrow of your bones: You are worthy of care.

I know that, at times, you may question your worth, especially when the world tells you that your needs are too great, your desires too complicated, or your feelings too intense. Perhaps you've spent so many years giving to others, caring for others, holding space for others, that you've forgotten to extend that same grace to yourself. Or maybe, in a world that often overlooks your complexity, you've convinced yourself that your needs don't matter, that your well-being is secondary.

Hear this, please: Your care matters. You matter. You deserve to be nurtured, supported, and loved with the same devotion and kindness you give to others. You deserve moments of rest, peace, and restoration. Your mind, your heart, your body, they all need and deserve the tenderness of care. You are not a burden. You are not too much to be cared for. You are *worthy* of care, just as you are.

It is easy to fall into the trap of believing that we must earn care or that we must first prove our worthiness. It is tempting to think that only after we've accomplished something, lived up to an ideal, or reached an unreachable standard, can we allow ourselves to be worthy of nurturing. But I want you to know that this is a lie. You are inherently worthy.

You are worthy to take time for yourself. You are worthy of rest, even if there's more work to be done. You are worthy of kindness, even when you feel you've faltered. You are worthy of compassion, especially in those moments when you feel misunderstood or alone. You are worthy of understanding, even when your complexity feels too much for the world to hold. Your needs, your feelings, and your soul are sacred, and they are deserving of respect, care, and love.

It may not always be easy to believe, but I ask you to try. When the doubts creep in, when the voices around you make you feel small or unworthy, gently remind yourself: I am worthy of care. I am worthy of rest. I am worthy of peace. These are not luxuries, they are rights. You have the right to live a life that honors your needs, to carve out moments for yourself, and to surround yourself with the love and care you so freely offer others.

You are not here to be invisible or to sacrifice your well-being for the sake of others. You are not here to carry the weight of the world without receiving the same love and support in return. It is not selfish to prioritize your needs. In fact, it is an act of radical self-love that will ripple out and inspire others to do the same.

I know that, as a neurodivergent soul, you often feel the weight of the world in ways others may not understand. Your sensitivity, your depth, your complexity, all these things make you *you*, and they are beautiful. But they also mean that you need care that honors your unique nature. You are not made to fit into the rigid boxes that society has set. You are meant to be honored for who you are, with all your colors and dimensions. This includes the right to be cared for in a way that aligns with your being.

Remember: You are worthy of care. Not because of what you do, not because of what you accomplish, but because of who you are. You are deserving of gentle love, of patience, of compassion, and of all the healing that this world has to offer.

So, my dear, allow yourself the grace to receive the care you so deeply deserve. Allow yourself permission to pause when you need rest. Allow yourself to ask for support when you need it. Your worth is not tied to your productivity. You are worthy, simply because you exist, and you deserve to be cherished, nurtured, and loved always.

With all my heart and unwavering support,

*Dianne*

## You Belong Here

Dear Beautiful Soul,

Know that you are not alone. Even if it has felt that way for far too long, even if the world has mirrored back confusion, judgment, or indifference, you are not, and never have been, alone.

There are others like you. Others who feel deeply and think in kaleidoscopes. Others whose nervous systems hum with the frequency of the unseen. Others who have spent years wondering if they were broken, only to discover they were simply wired for something deeper, truer, more luminous than the world was ready to understand.

I see you. I see the strength it takes to move through a world not built for your rhythm. The quiet courage of getting out of bed when everything inside you is overstimulated or shut down. The deep ache for connection and the fear that your full truth might be too much.

I want you to know that you are not too much. You are never too little. You were never meant to contort yourself to fit in. You were born to belong fully, freely, without needing to explain your brilliance or dilute your essence.

There is nothing wrong with you. The way your brain fires, the way your heart feels, the way your senses sing or protest, none of it is a mistake. It is not disorder; it is design. You are not here to follow the narrow path. You are here to bring light to the wild, beautiful, uncharted ones.

And while the world may not always know how to receive you, there is a growing constellation of kindred souls, people who *do* get it, who are walking their own neurodivergent paths with tenderness and fire. You are part of this community, this movement, this quiet revolution of authenticity.

You are not alone. In your longing, your brilliance, your sensitivity, your struggle, and your joy, you are seen. You are held. And you are deeply, profoundly worthy of love, rest, care, and belonging exactly as you are.

Let this be your reminder: you do not have to earn your place. You already belong.

With all my heart,

*Dianne*

## You Are Not Alone

Dear Fellow Neurodivergent Soul,

Welcome home. I can imagine your journey has been anything but simple. Perhaps it's been layered with confusion, intense emotion, deep perception, and moments where the world felt too small for the bigness of your being. Maybe you've spent years trying to *fit in*, in systems, in roles, in relationships that were never built with your sensitivity or brilliance in mind. I want you to know: your effort has always been seen. And now, you don't have to strive to belong. You already do. You belong here. Just as you are.

What you've carried is not a burden, it's a constellation. Your mind that moves fast and far. Your emotions that surge with color and complexity. Your imagination that never sleeps. These are not flaws to be corrected. These are sacred signatures of your soul. The world may not have been fluent in your language, but that doesn't make your song any less true. You were never broken. You were always building something extraordinary, something only *you* could build.

Here, you are not too much. You are a prism. And all of your light, every facet, every frequency, is welcome. I see you. I know the effort it's taken to walk through this world with your full sensitivity intact. I know how lonely it can feel to carry a unique form of knowing, to see patterns others miss, to feel things others dismiss. And I know, deeply, that your way of being *is the medicine* this world needs most.

You don't need to edit yourself to be worthy of love, success, joy, or rest. You simply need to return to yourself. And that return begins now.

With tenderness, brilliance, and a fierce knowing,

*Michelle*

# Glossary

**ADHD (Attention-Deficit/Hyperactivity Disorder)**
A neurodevelopmental condition involving differences in attention, energy regulation, and executive functioning. For many, it shows up as creative problem-solving, emotional intensity, and a drive for interest and novelty rather than simple distractibility.

**Autism / Autistic**
A neurodevelopmental identity describing a way of processing the world that includes deep focus, sensory sensitivity, and unique communication and social styles. Autism is a divergent design.

**Burnout**
A state of deep emotional, mental, or physical exhaustion. For neurodivergent people, burnout often results from masking, sensory overload, or ignoring your unique needs and rhythm.

**Cycles of Shutdown**
Natural periods where your nervous system requires restoration. Shutdown is wisdom from within, asking for space, safety, and recalibration.

**Emotional Regulation**
The ability to navigate big emotions in a way that honors your neurobiology and soul. This often includes sensory tools, rituals, and compassionate awareness rather than suppression.

**Executive Function**
Mental processes that manage planning, working memory, time, and attention. Many neurodivergent individuals experience executive function differently and may benefit from alternative approaches or accommodations.

### Giftedness
A deeply sensitive and perceptive way of being. Giftedness includes intellectual capacity and also emotional depth, spiritual awareness, and a hunger for authenticity and meaning.

### Hyperfocus
An immersive state of concentration, common in ADHD and gifted individuals, where time disappears and focus is intense. It can be a gift when supported with rhythm and regulation.

### Intense Sensitivities
A term coined in *Someone Gets Me* referring to gifted individuals with overexcitabilities as described by Dabrowski coupled with intuition and empathic sensitivities.

### Masking
The effort of hiding or minimizing your neurodivergent traits to appear more "typical." Masking often leads to burnout and internal disconnection. Unmasking is part of healing.

### Misattunement
Refers to a lack of emotional connection or a mismatch between what someone expresses and how they are understood by another person, particularly in close relationships

### Neurodivergent / Neurodivergence
A term describing individuals whose brains function differently than the cultural norm. This includes people with ADHD, autism, learning differences, giftedness, and more. Neurodivergence is not something to fix—it is something to understand and honor.

### Overstimulation / Sensory Overload
A state of overwhelm caused by too much sensory input. For neurodivergent souls, this can be triggered by light, sound, texture, crowds, or even emotion, and often requires soothing or withdrawal.

### Polyvagal Theory
A model for understanding how the nervous system responds to

safety and threat. Knowing your "state", whether you're in fight, flight, freeze, or connection can help you care for yourself more wisely.

**Recovery**
A multidimensional healing process that includes physical, emotional, and spiritual restoration. Recovery here refers to healing from substance use, trauma, burnout, or medical challenges in a way that honors your neurodivergent nature. Recovery means "to feel better".

**Rituals for Regulation**
Intentional practices that help calm, center, and energize the nervous system. These might include journaling, breathwork, movement, or creative expression.

**Safe Inner Sanctuary**
A sacred internal space you cultivate through imagery, ritual, or intention, a place where your soul can rest and restore, no matter what is happening externally.

**Sensory Sensitivity**
A heightened awareness or reactivity to sensory input such as sound, light, textures, or emotions. It's not a weakness; it's a form of deep perception.

**Shame Layering**
The internalized belief that your differences make you defective. Shame often builds from repeated misunderstanding, rejection, or pressure to conform. Releasing it is part of coming home to yourself.

**Soul Care**
Deep, intentional nourishment of your whole self-emotional, energetic, intuitive, and spiritual. It's the foundation of a life that supports your sensitivity, rhythm, and truth.

**Twice Exceptional (2e)**
Describes individuals who are both gifted and neurodivergent. These souls often experience both exceptional strengths and profound

challenges and may be misdiagnosed or overlooked by traditional systems.

**Unmasking**
The courageous act of letting go of roles, coping mechanisms, and false identities that were used to survive. It is a sacred return to your true self, free, whole, and visible.

APPENDIX

# A RESOURCE GUIDE FOR THE NEURODIVERGENT SOUL

This collection of resources is designed to support your ongoing journey. Whether you are seeking deeper knowledge, meaningful community, or compassionate tools for daily life, these offerings provide pathways to continued care, clarity, and connection. These resources are not prescriptive checklists, they are invitations. Take what resonates. Leave what doesn't. Add your own discoveries. Most of all, let your inner wisdom guide you as you continue honoring your path.

**Books by Dianne A. Allen**

These works form the heart of the message carried throughout *Care for the Neurodivergent Soul*. They are written for the gifted, the intense, the sensitive, and the seekers who long to be seen and understood.

- *Someone Gets Me.* A compassionate guide for gifted, ADHD, and autistic adults navigating a world not designed for them. This book offers validation, soulful insight, and practical tools for healing and thriving.
- *Where Do You Fit In?* Written especially for those who feel "different on purpose," this book provides clarity and direction

for gifted souls seeking connection without compromising who they are.
- *Hope Realized.* A collection of daily reflections with journaling prompts for those who are healing their heart, soul, and inner knowing.
- *Meditations for Visionary Leaders.* A collection of daily reflections for those who lead from the heart, soul, and inner knowing.
- *The Loneliness Cure: A Guide to Contentment.* Explores the hidden struggles of intelligent, sensitive, and gifted adults who often feel out of place despite their external success. Offers practical guidance and hopeful reflection on cultivating true belonging.
- *How to Quit Anything in 5 Simple Steps.* Seeks to explore ways to become free of addictive patterns using a multifaceted model for regaining life balance and freedom.

## Further Reading for the Neurodivergent Soul
- *The Divergent Mind*, by Jenara Nerenberg. A groundbreaking book on neurodivergent women and nonbinary individuals and their experience of sensitivity, creativity, and intuition.
- *Neurotribes*, by Steve Silberman. An expansive history of autism and the evolution of neurodiversity. Offers cultural context and advocacy insights.
- *Drama of the Gifted Child*, by Alice Miller. A classic on the emotional challenges of gifted children and the importance of reclaiming the authentic self.
- *Quiet: The Power of Introverts in a World That Can't Stop Talking*, by Susan Cain. A powerful resource for sensitive and introspective souls navigating a noisy world.
- *Uniquely Human*, by Barry M. Prizant, PhDShifts the lens on autism from pathology to humanity, offering compassionate understanding.
- *Neurodiversity Playbook: How Neurodivergent People Can Crack

*the Code of Living in a Neurotypical World*, by Matthew Zakreski PsyD. This book represents a summation of a decade's worth of therapy, research, workshops, and presentations around the unique aspects of social-emotional development in the neurodivergent community.
- *Gifted and Distractible: Understanding, Supporting, and Advocating for Your Twice Exceptional Child*, by Julie F. Skolnick. A practical, research-based guide that demystifies giftedness and learning differences to help "twice exceptional" children thrive.

## Podcasts
- *Someone Gets Me with Dianne A. Allen*. A podcast for gifted, sensitive, and neurodivergent individuals exploring authenticity, intuition, creativity, and leadership. Features interviews, reflections, and practical tools for soulful living. Listen on Apple Podcasts or Spotify
- *The Neurodiversity Podcast (formerly The Mind Matters Podcast)*. Hosted by Emily Kircher-Morris, LPC, this show offers expert conversations on twice-exceptionality, giftedness, ADHD, autism, and education.
- *Uniquely Human: The Podcast.* Hosted by Dr. Barry Prizant and Dave Finch, this podcast explores autism and neurodiversity with warmth, insight, and humor.
- *The Divergent Mind Podcast.* Conversations about living and thriving as a neurodivergent adult, with emphasis on self-discovery, boundaries, and identity.

## Websites and Organizations
- Visions Applied. Home of Dianne A. Allen's mentoring, books, and programs. Offers one-on-one guidance, soulful resources, and community for gifted and neurodivergent adults. www.visionsapplied.com
- With Understanding Comes Calm. Offers resources and community for parents and adults navigating giftedness,

twice-exceptionality, and mental health. www.withunderstandingcomescalm.com
- Gifted and Distractible (With Bright & Quirky). Offers resources and community for parents and adults navigating giftedness, twice-exceptionality, and mental health. www.brightandquirky.com
- SENG (Supporting Emotional Needs of the Gifted). A leading organization focused on the social and emotional needs of gifted individuals. Offers parent groups, adult resources, and events. www.sengifted.org
- ADDA (Attention Deficit Disorder Association). Offers resources for adults with ADHD, including webinars, virtual support groups, and advocacy tools. www.add.org
- AuDHD.org. A hub for those who identify as both autistic and ADHD, providing affirming resources, blog posts, and lived experience narratives. www.audhd.org

**Tools & Sensory-Friendly Resources**
- **Loop Earplugs**. Designed for sound sensitivity; these stylish and effective earplugs help regulate overwhelming environments. www.loopearplugs.com
- **Time Timer®** A visual timer that helps with executive functioning, time-blindness, and transitions, particularly useful for ADHD individuals. www.timetimer.com
- **Insight Timer (App)**. A free meditation and mindfulness app with guided practices, music, and tools for sleep and nervous system regulation. www.insighttimer.com
- **EmWave by HeartMath**. A biofeedback tool that supports emotional regulation and coherence by tracking heart rhythms. www.heartmath.com

**Reflection and Integration Tools (Printable or Editable)**
These tools are available through *Care for the Neurodivergent Soul* or via the Visions Applied resource hub:

- **Energy Map Worksheet**. A one-page guide to help track and honor your energy rhythms throughout the day or week.
- **Daily Rhythm Template**. Designed with neurodivergent needs in mind, this tool helps you build a sustainable, sensory-aware daily flow.
- **Coming Home to Your Inner Compass**. A short, guided practice for reconnecting with your intuitive self and calming the nervous system.
- **Reflection Journal Prompts**. Printable prompts for deeper self-exploration, aligned with themes throughout the book.

You are not alone in this transformation. Others have walked and are walking their own neurodivergent soul path. Together, we remember how to live fully, love freely, and lead from the truth of who we are.

# EPILOGUE

# A RETURN TO THE SELF

You've made it to the end, or perhaps the beginning of a new way of living. This book is not a conclusion. It is a compass, a soft lantern in the dark, a reminder that your soul was never in need of fixing. Only remembering.

If you've felt seen in these pages, it's because your truth already lived within you. These words simply offered a mirror. Along the way, we've walked through many tangled paths of misunderstanding, overwork, shame, and loneliness. We've stopped to rest in moments of joy, found rhythm in our inner compass, and learned to translate our unique way of being into a life of meaning and connection.

You are not too much. You are not too little. You are precisely the shape and texture of soul this world needs.

The systems around us may never fully understand what it means to be wired differently. We are not here for their approval. We are here to live with integrity, to reclaim our energy, to speak our truth with clarity, and to belong fully to ourselves. Our brilliance may never fit inside neat boxes or flowcharts. That is not our concern. Our calling is to show up with courage and care.

I hope you leave these pages carrying strategies to manage yourself more efficiently, rather holding deeper permission to be yourself more freely.

There is no finish line in caring for your neurodivergent soul. There is only deepening, softening, and returning again and again to your truth. You are seen. You are sacred. You are sovereign. Keep going.

With you in spirit and soul,
*Dianne A. Allen, MA*

## About the Author

**Dianne A. Allen, MA** is a visionary mentor, intuitive guide, and ambassador for gifted and neurodivergent adults, families and teams. With decades of experience as a counselor, speaker, and author, Dianne blends emotional wisdom with grounded expertise to help others reconnect with their innate brilliance. As the founder of *Someone Gets Me* and *Visions Applied*, she empowers sensitive, creative, and high-achieving individuals to embrace their full selves and thrive in a world that often misunderstands them.

Known for her compassionate clarity and soulful insight, Dianne's work bridges the seen and unseen, the scientific and the spiritual. Her writing, speaking, and mentoring illuminate a path of deep self-trust, restoration, and lasting transformation. Through *Care for the Neurodivergent Soul*, she offers both a sanctuary and a guidebook for those longing to feel seen, heard, and fully alive.

**Connect with Dianne:**
www.MsDianneAllen.com
www.VisionsApplied.com

**Previous Books include:**
*How to Quit Anything in 5 Simple Steps*
*The Loneliness Cure*
*Daily Meditations for Visionary Leaders*
*Hope Realized*
*Where Do You Fit In?*
*Someone Gets Me*

www.ingramcontent.com/pod-product-compliance
Lightning Source LLC
Chambersburg PA
CBHW050327010526
44119CB00050B/703